GOLF
MAGAZINE'S
Private Lessons

── EDITED BY ──

JAMES A. FRANK

Stephen Greene Press/Pelham Books

THE STEPHEN GREENE PRESS/PELHAM BOOKS

Published by the Penguin Group
Viking Penguin, a division of Penguin Books USA Inc., 40 West 23rd Street,
　New York, New York 10010, U.S.A.
Penguin Books Ltd, 27 Wrights Lane, London W8 5TZ, England
Penguin Books Australia Ltd, Ringwood, Victoria, Australia
Penguin Books Canada Ltd, 2801 John Street, Markham, Ontario, Canada L3R 1B4
Penguin Books (N.Z.) Ltd, 182–190 Wairau Road, Auckland 10, New Zealand

Penguin Books Ltd, Registered Offices: Harmondsworth, Middlesex, England

First published in 1990 by The Stephen Greene Press/Pelham Books

Distributed by Viking Penguin, a division of Penguin Books USA Inc.

10 9 8 7 6 5 4 3 2 1

The contents of this book first appeared in *Golf* Magazine as installments of the
column, "Private Lessons" and are reprinted by arrangement with Times Mirror
Magazines, Inc.

Library of Congress Cataloging-in-Publication Data
Golf magazine's private lessons / edited by James A. Frank.
　　　p.　　cm.
　　Compilation of the best lessons from Golf magazine's column
　Private lessons.
　　ISBN 0-8289-0798-6
　　1. Golf.　I. Frank, James A.　II. Golf magazine.
　GV966.G5458　1989
　796.352'05—dc20　　　　　　　　　　　　　　　　　　89-29808
　　　　　　　　　　　　　　　　　　　　　　　　　　　　CIP

Printed in the United States of America

CONTENTS

INTRODUCTION

Since the first golf instruction manual was published more than 100 years ago, teachers of the game have treated their students like clones. In almost every book, article, and videotape produced to help you play better golf, the instruction wasn't aimed at you at all, but at some mythical "average" golfer.

For years, the editors of *Golf* Magazine followed much the same thinking. In preparing our articles, we tried to address as many golfers as possible with a single theory. When we'd offer a new way to swing, we would have to begin by convincing ourselves that a 65-year-old retiree would have no more trouble picking it up than the 25-year-old long-ball hitter, knowing perfectly well that that wasn't true. The confines of magazine pages simply didn't allow much customization for the many different types of golfer we knew existed.

In 1985, the editors of *Golf* Magazine set out to change all that. Nagging at the back of our minds for years had been the knowledge that all golfers are *not* alike, and that there was no "average golfer." We saw that among our staff, we saw that in every weekend foursome, we even saw it among the pros. Every golfer has special needs, and we wanted to address those needs by offering instruction articles that would deal directly with his, or her, problems.

Before we could write a single specialized word, we had to determine how many different types of golfer existed. A survey was sent to thousands of *Golf* Magazine readers. In it we asked them about their age, height, weight, and handicap, then probed for more specific responses: How long do you hit your driver? Your 5-iron? In one round, how many greens do you hit in regulation? How many three-putts? What is the best aspect of your game? The worst? What shot or situation scares you the most? In all, we posed four pages of questions and were rewarded with pages of detail about how golfers *really* play.

Armed with the responses, we looked for similarities that would allow us to split golfers into categories based on skill. We had some suspicions going in: It was obvious that we'd see good players at one end of the spectrum, the new and lesser-skilled players at the other. But we were less sure—and more curious—about the remainder, the masses who usually get tagged with the "average" label. What we found was that they divided into two groups, wild long-hitters and straight short-hitters. (Yes, there probably are a few wild short-hitters and straight long-hitters, but their needs are well served by the high handicapper and low handicapper categories, respectively.)

After months of researching, analyzing, and massaging, we debuted "Private Lessons" in February 1986, and unveiled the four golfer-types with descriptions that covered more than 90 percent of our readers:

- Low Handicapper: You have a sound all-around game, but you'd like to shave those last few strokes off your handicap.
- Power Hitter: You hit the ball a long way, but rarely as straight as you want. Your game needs control and consistency.
- Straight Hitter: You keep the ball in play most of the time, but a lack of distance puts pressure on your game.
- High Handicapper: You have the potential for a better game but first need to solve some fundamental problems.

Each month, "Private Lessons" offers four personalized articles, one to each golfer-type. That means 12 a year for each group, a total of 48 lessons a year for the last four years.

In compiling this "best of" "Private Lessons," I had to choose from nearly 200 articles. I've looked for the pieces that speak most directly to each group's needs and for a selection of articles that will give each golfer-type the most help. So while the Low Handicapper won't be told to change his already successful swing, he will read about strategy and advanced methods for getting the most out of his game. At the other extreme, the High Handicapper can count on a little bit of everything, from getting started with the proper fundamentals to handling the trouble he is sure to find. The Power Hitter is offered advice on scrambling from off the fairway (where his wayward shots are likely to land), while the Straight Hitter learns how to hit for more distance.

Although "Private Lessons" are designed as individualized instruction, you shouldn't assume that the methods offered to other golfer-types won't help you. I encourage you to look at all four sections of this book. But I suggest that you start with the lessons in the chapter most appropriate to the way you play, and when you do look at other chapters, remember that some of the shots and skills required may be outside your present level. As you improve, refer back to the earlier lessons for a "refresher course."

With "Private Lessons" or any golf instruction, what you get out of it is only as good as what you put in. There are no magic answers or short cuts. You have to practice if you wish to lower your scores. But if the hundreds of thank-you letters and success stories we've received are any indication, I'm sure you'll benefit by reading "Private Lessons" and practicing what they preach.

James A. Frank
Executive Editor, *Golf* Magazine
September, 1989

——ACKNOWLEDGMENTS——

"Private Lessons" grew out of a number of *Golf* Magazine editorial meetings held in early 1985. The creators were magazine Editor George Peper, Senior Editor of Instruction John Andrisani, and myself. The instruction department was responsible for the original manuscripts and generation of ideas to perpetuate the series. Associate Editor Kenneth Van Kampen joined the staff in October 1986 and has been the principal shepherd for "Private Lessons" ever since.

Not to be forgotten is artist Barry Ross, whose drawings and layouts have given this series its unique identity and beauty.

For helping to turn a collection of magazine articles into a book, credit must be shared with the Business Development Staff of Times Mirror Magazines—Vice President Gertrud Borchardt, assistant Erika Yarmoff, and intern Karyn Richman.

—J.A.F.

High Handicapper

You have the potential for a better game but first need to solve some fundamental problems.

Every golfer begins as a high handicapper, struggling to break 100 and develop some consistency. The high handicapper can benefit from instruction in every part of the game, but is most in need of help with the basics of the swing—starting with how to set-up to the ball and move the club. Therefore, most of the articles in this section deal with the fundamentals, from taking a stance to making a sound swing.

Of course, until the high handicapper improves, he's going to visit every part of the course, and particularly the hazards. Articles on trouble shots and smart recoveries—from sand, rough, and uneven lies—should help. Eventually the lesser-skilled player will find himself on and around the green with a chance to lower his score through chipping and putting. These areas are not neglected.

More than anything else, however, the high handicapper needs to develop confidence. That comes only with practice and regular play, building familiarity with the equipment and its uses, and understanding that good golf demands time and hard work. The articles in this chapter provide a sound introduction.

DON'T REACH
FOR TROUBLE

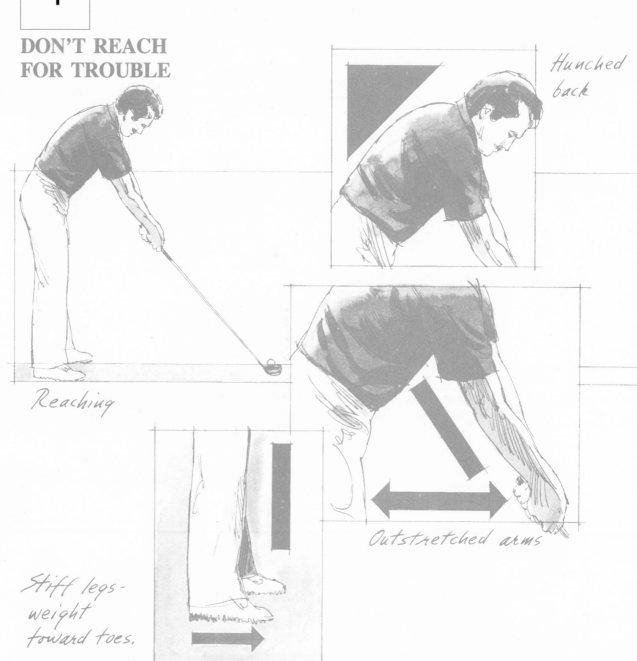

Reaching

Hunched back

Outstretched arms

Stiff legs-
weight
toward toes.

You can almost always tell the high handicapper from the low handicapper before either swings a club. How? By checking their postures when they address the ball.

The most revealing view of a player's posture is from behind the target line. While the fine player appears relaxed and well-balanced, the high handicapper seems tense and strained. More

often than not, he's standing too far from the ball, and his body seems to know it. It's possible to stand too close to the ball as well, but that's a less common flaw. Think about how you feel at address. Is this you? Legs stiff and weight toward your toes; back hunched over at a fairly severe angle; and worst, both arms are stretched out to their maximum reach.

Reaching for the ball probably makes you feel powerful. But it's useless power, a tension in your arms and upper back that will not help develop clubhead speed. In fact, reaching too far tightens the muscles so they can't move as smoothly and quickly as if they were hanging naturally.

Reaching also puts the right shoulder and arm in a dominant position, stretched straight out

Bend slightly from waist.

Correct Posture

Flexed knees – weight centered over feet.

Arms hang naturally, right elbow bent.

rather than having the right elbow bent and the arm folded in toward the side. This setup encourages an outside-in chopping motion with the right side that guarantees a slice. Finally, reaching too far causes a loss of balance. You might fall toward the ball during the swing, a common fault.

BEND KNEES, LET ARMS HANG
How do you find the right pos-ture for you? Try this. Without a club or a ball to influence you, practice your address posture. Flex your knees as if you're going to sit in a chair. Bend slightly from the waist, like a tennis player waiting to return a serve. Next, let your arms hang naturally and ten-sion-free and bring your palms together, keeping a six-to-eight-inch clearance between your hands and the front of your trou-sers. Slide your right hand a little toward the fingers of your left (as if holding a club). This is where your hands should be and how your posture should look and feel when playing.

Follow this same setup proce-dure with a club in hand. Your body will feel "loose," which means you'll be better prepared to execute a smooth-flowing swing.

2

SMART ROUGH RECOVERIES

You know from experience that you hit a high percentage of tee shots into the rough. What you do once you're there determines whether you take a round-ruining big number or save par or bogey. Here's how to play it smart—and safe—out of rough.

ASSESS THE LIE

Let's say you're in the rough and at least 180 yards from the green. Even from the fairway, you'd need a fine wood shot to get home.

Occasionally, you'll catch a lie in the rough with the ball sitting up so you can go after it with a lofted wood. The mistake you often make, though, is to take the same club from a terrible lie as you do from a good one, thinking you might just pull off a miracle shot. That's when you leave the ball right there or hit it into worse trouble.

To get out of trouble and back in play, first determine which club will get you out safely. If your ball is really lying deep in the grass, accept the fact that you can't get to the green. Realize that your best move may be to go with a 7-, 8-, 9-iron or even a wedge.

Your goal is to get back in the fairway, leaving you a simple third shot. Don't think that by doing this you're playing "chicken." You're playing smart. When Tour pros are buried in U.S. Open rough, they do the same thing.

CHOKE DOWN, SWING SHORT

Pick the club you know will get you out. Address the ball with a square clubface, out of the center of your stance, putting more weight than usual on your left side. These adjustments help you hit down, which counters the muffling effect of the grass on club and ball.

Choke down on the club at least an inch: This gives you more control, and the narrower clubhead arc to dig the ball from the rough. Swing the club up mainly with your arms to no further than a three-quarter position. You'll stay centered to help ensure a solid hit.

DRIVE DOWN

Don't try to scoop the shot out. Pull down aggressively with your left arm to retain maximum leverage while the clubhead's downswing arc remains steep.

Keep your left hand and arm moving down and through the shot as long as possible. Your follow-through will be retarded a bit by the impact of the club with the ground, so don't worry about finishing high.

Aim a bit to the right of where you want the ball to finish; the grass will catch the hosel of the club somewhat, closing the clubface so the ball goes a little left. Also, the ball will come out slightly lower and with more roll than normal with a lofted iron.

With proper club selection and execution you can put the ball safely in the fairway. You'll be in a good position and in a good frame of mind for your pitch to the pin. From your earlier position, par or bogey is a good score.

Choke down and make an upright, three-quarter swing.

Pull down firmly with the left hand in control and drive through the ball.

Play ball back.

3

GETTING FROM
PRACTICE TEE
TO GOLF COURSE

How often have you heard a playing partner in the throes of a bad round say that he'd been hitting the ball well on the practice tee? How often have you played poorly after hitting shots solidly and accurately on the range? Take heart; many golfers share the frustration of not being able to bring the good practice shots to the course.

Have you ever hit good shots on the practice range, only to flounder on the course?

PSYCHOLOGICAL FACTOR

Obviously, the problem isn't physical: You've proven that on the range. It could be that you're "over-thinking" on the course. On the range, you're free to blast one ball after another without worrying about the consequences of a bad shot. When you think less and let instincts take over, you perform better physically. Not that you never hit a bad shot on the practice range—far from it. But when you do, it's quickly forgotten. So it's psychologically less taxing to hit practice balls.

Compare that to actual play. Suppose you've sliced your drive on the first hole. Standing on the second tee, it will be hard to forget your first tee shot. But you have to put it out of your mind.

Try this: If you hit the ball well in practice, you must have had streaks of hitting several good shots in a row. Imagine yourself back in one of those streaks, having just hit a string of four good drives. Recalling that will help eliminate negative thinking and replace it with confidence.

TIME FACTOR

Another difference between the course and the practice tee is the amount of time between shots. It's easy to find a "groove" on the range because you can hit shot after shot, whereas on the course you have to wait, sometimes a few minutes. To regain your form after a delay, imagine hitting a shot while you take a practice swing. Again, pretend you're back on the range and take another practice swing, pretending to hit another ball. Then step up to the real ball and fire away.

MISCONCEPTION FACTOR

Were you actually hitting the ball that well on the range? If you weren't hitting to a specific target, you don't really know how accurate your shots were. They may have been solid, but it's possible they weren't on target. It's easy to get the feeling that the ball is going great when hitting into a wide-open space. For a more realistic picture, narrow your sights: Pick two target points to represent the boundaries of an imaginary fairway and green and a single point for an imaginary pin.

Use your practice swing to imagine hitting a shot back on the range.

You must put a poor shot from the past out of your mind.

4

CONQUER THE LONG LAG

There are certain areas of your game that you can improve a lot faster than others. Learning to lag your long putts consistently close enough for a sure two-putt is one of the best ways to trim strokes quickly.

USE SOME WRIST BREAK

If you analyze why you three-putt or even four-putt those 40-50 footers, you know the problem is almost always distance, not direction. You may leave the putt 12 feet short or knock it the same distance past, but you rarely stroke it more than three feet off line. Obviously, you must develop a more sensitive feel for distance in your stroke.

Start with the way you stroke the long putt. On short- or middle-length putts you might have success using an arm-and-shoulder stroke, keeping the wrists firm and the putterhead low to the ground and accelerating through the ball. On the long ones, though, this stroke may feel a bit wooden. You might find it hard to reach the hole without using some wrist.

When you face a long putt, particularly one that's uphill, make a backstroke that's long enough to get the ball to the hole without jerking the club back through the ball. Let the wrists hinge naturally so that the putterblade comes well

Let a slight wrist break lift putterhead well off the ground.

Take the putter back far enough so there's no need to jerk it back through.

off the ground at the top of the stroke. On the follow-through, match the length of the back-swing, again letting the wrists hinge slightly, with the putterhead coming well off the ground.

SHOOT FOR THE CIRCLE

When preparing for a long putt, study direction first, then focus your attention on how hard you need to hit the ball to get it close. On putts of 40 feet or more, your goal is simple: Make the ball finish within a three-foot circle around the cup.

Walk quickly along the line of your putt, noting any uphill or downhill slope and the length of the grass. The grass around the cup will be more worn than at any other point along the line of your putt, so the ball will pick up a little speed there; you may not notice that if you study the putt only from around the ball.

Some players find it helpful to walk to the midpoint of a long putt, take a practice stroke from there and double the force of that stroke for the actual putt. Breaking the distance into halves can give you greater confidence than trying to get the feel of a rolling 50-footer all at once.

Most high handicappers also tend to underestimate how much an upslope or downslope affects the roll of putt. With a long uphiller, you may have to think a bit "long" to get it inside that three-foot radius. On a downhill putt of the same length, you may be surprised at how much farther the ball rolls than it would if the surface were level.

Spend a good bit of your prac-tice time working on those long, tough putts. Alternate between long uphill, downhill and sidehill putts. It's a good idea to putt only one ball to each hole. That way, you'll have to adjust your force and your aim with each stroke. This will help you when you face vari-ous types of long putts out on the course.

Even if you err a bit on the line, with the right distance you'll still finish "in the circle."

5

VARY YOUR
BALL POSITION

Ball position: Should you play the ball from the same position in your stance for every shot? Or should you move the ball forward and back as the shots vary?

Experienced players who have grooved their swings so the bottom of the arc is always at the same spot can comfortably place the ball in the same spot—usually off the left heel—on every shot. But if consistency is not your hallmark, try playing the ball farther back in your stance on middle and short irons. You will find it easier to make better contact.

For middle irons, address the ball about one ball width inside the left heel.

Setting up with the hands ahead allows you to hit the shot with the clubface at the proper angle and loft.

Hands ahead of ball

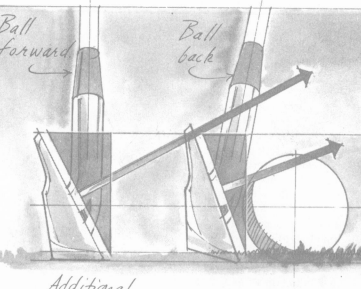

Ball forward

Ball back

Additional loft

True loft

FIND THE BOTTOM OF YOUR ARC

Before you start experimenting with ball position, locate the bottom of your swing arc with the higher-numbered clubs. Take three practice swings with a 5-iron, taking a divot as if you were hitting a ball. Note where the divots begin. That's the bottom of your swing arc, and where you should position the ball at address.

If you're having trouble finding an average spot, try these: For middle irons, place the ball one ball-width behind the left heel; for the short irons, start with the ball two ball-widths back. Experiment with those positions until you've zeroed in on your ideals.

POSITION FOR BETTER CONTACT

Changing ball position promotes better contact because you'll strike the ball first then the turf, instead of the other way around, and you'll make a descending blow. Besides eliminating the chance of hitting the ground before the ball and possibly throwing the clubface out of line, you also will put more backspin on a properly struck shot.

Playing the ball back in your stance also places your hands ahead of the clubhead at address, so you take advantage of the club's loft. If the ball is too far forward, you may tend to set up with the hands even with or behind the clubhead, tilting the face up. This adds loft to the club, making the shot go higher and shorter than expected. Setting up with the hands ahead encourages leading with them through the downswing. You'll make contact with the clubface in a proper position—at the angle and loft it was designed for—so you'll be rewarded with the most distance and best trajectory.

For short irons, address the ball about two ball widths inside the left heel.

Playing the ball back makes it easier to strike it first and then the turf.

Descending blow

Maximum backspin.

6

READ THE SHAPE OF YOUR SHOTS

You tend to hit too many shots that don't fly straight. Do you know what determines a shot's direction? To improve, you must understand what causes specific shot shapes so you can begin making the necessary adjustments.

DOWNSWING PATH + CLUBFACE ALIGNMENT = SHOT

The shot you hit is the result of the club's downswing path coupled with the clubface alignment at impact. The downswing path determines the ball's initial direction. Face alignment at impact determines spin and how the ball will curve.

THE 11 SHOTS IN GOLF

Once struck, there are 11 ways a ball can fly. The "straight" ball (1), is the result of a down-the-line path and a square clubface at impact. Combine the straight path with a slightly open clubface for a "fade" (2), which begins straight then bends slightly from left to right. A straight path with a slightly closed clubface creates a "draw" (3), starting straight and bending slightly right to left.

The three shots above won't hurt you. But if the path is straight and the clubface wide open, you'll put too much sidespin on the ball and hit a "slice" (4), which starts straight but curves way

right. A closed face causes a "hook" (5), which starts straight, then bends far left.

If the clubhead path is inside-out, the ball starts out to the right. Pair that with a square clubface (square to the path, not the target line), and the result is a ball hit straight right—a "push" (6). A closed face will give you a "round-house hook" (7) that starts to the right before making a big turn back to the left. If the clubface is open, the "push-slice" (8) starts right and curves even farther to the right.

An outside-in path starts the ball to the left. Marry it with a square clubface and you'll get a "pull" (9), which sails dead left. Open the clubface and you'll hit the common "pull-slice" (10), which starts left and curves back right, sacrificing distance. Close the clubface and you'll hit a "pull-hook" (11), starting left and curving farther left.

Watch your shots closely and note how they fly. You now can figure out your clubhead path and face alignment, the first stage in correcting them.

Down-the-line Path

Ball Path

Downswing Path

Square

Straight

Fade (slightly open face)

Slice (very open)

Spin

Open

Fade and Slice

Hook (very closed face)

Draw (slightly closed)

Closed

Draw and Hook

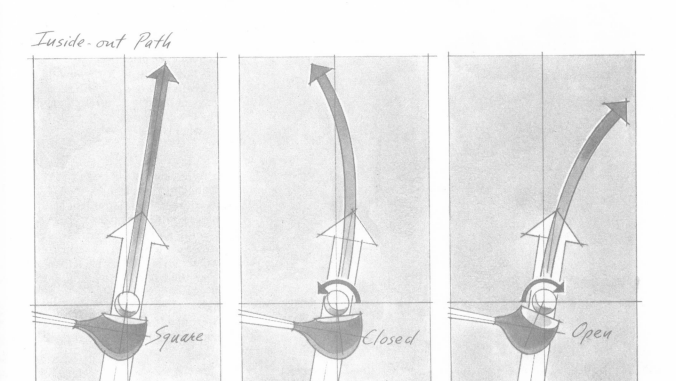

Inside-out Path

Push — Square

Round-house Hook — Closed

Push-slice — Open

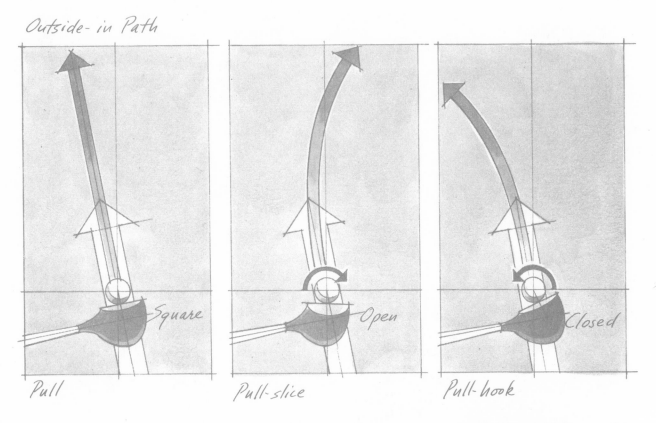

Outside-in Path

Pull — Square

Pull-slice — Open

Pull-hook — Closed

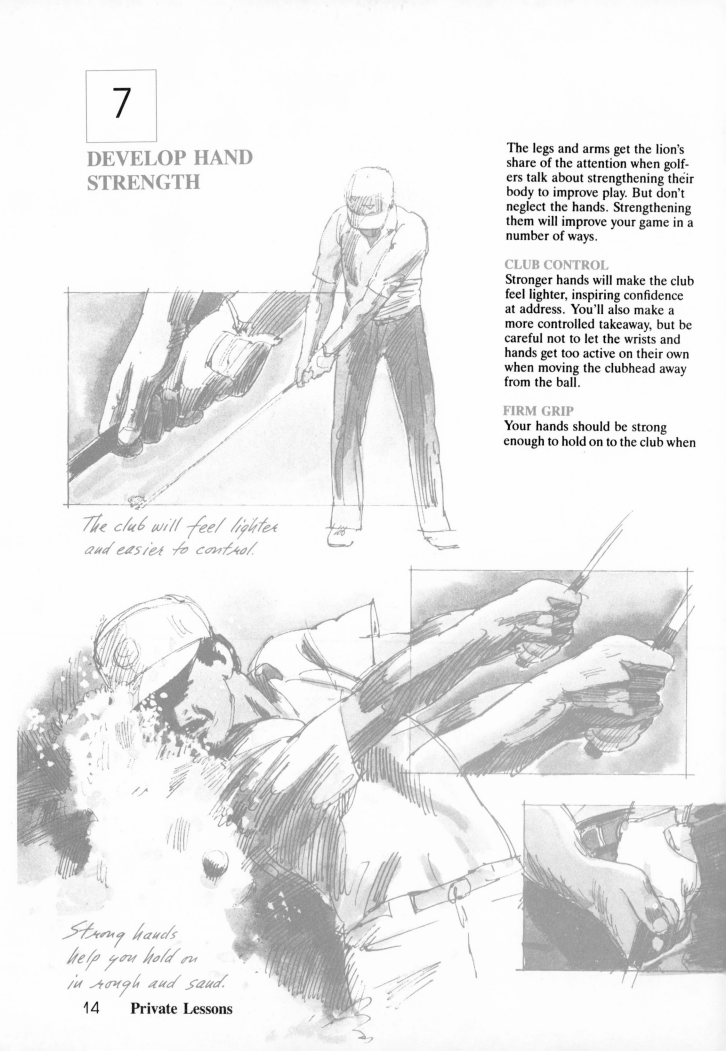

7

DEVELOP HAND STRENGTH

The legs and arms get the lion's share of the attention when golfers talk about strengthening their body to improve play. But don't neglect the hands. Strengthening them will improve your game in a number of ways.

CLUB CONTROL
Stronger hands will make the club feel lighter, inspiring confidence at address. You'll also make a more controlled takeaway, but be careful not to let the wrists and hands get too active on their own when moving the clubhead away from the ball.

FIRM GRIP
Your hands should be strong enough to hold on to the club when

The club will feel lighter and easier to control.

Strong hands help you hold on in rough and sand.

hitting from trouble—especially exploding from a buried lie in sand or coming out of deep rough. Strong hands will reduce the twisting of the clubhead, keeping shots on line. A firmer grip also helps your iron play since the hands and wrists don't break down at contact. As a result, contact will feel more solid, and you may pick up a few yards.

SOLID SHORT GAME

On the green, power in the hands gives you better control of the blade along the target line. The same goes for chipping: More control over the clubhead means better chances of hitting the ball on the line you want and with the force you want. As hand strength builds, guard against gripping too tightly, which cuts feel. Your fingertips should rest lightly on the club.

More clubhead control.

Hit and Stop Drill

Take two long irons or a weighted club and grip firmly. Make a slow, smooth backswing, swing down, but try to stop the club with your hands as soon as the club passes the impact point. It will feel awkward at first, but you'll get the hang of it. Repeat until you get a burning sensation in your forearms. You'll notice an increase in hand-strength almost immediately.

8

PLAY YOUR LEVEL BEST FROM HILLY LIES

Set up with line of hips and shoulders parallel to slope.

No matter how flat a course first appears, you'll eventually end up having to hit the ball off a slope. It may be an uphill, downhill or side-hill lie, and any one of them will frustrate the player who doesn't know how to play them or understand their effects on ball flight.

The key to hitting the ball in each of these circumstances is adjusting your address position so you make contact at the bottom of the swing arc. Couple that with an understanding of how the ball will bend as a result of these adjustments and you can turn a tough situation to your advantage.

UPHILL/DOWNHILL

To get into the proper address position to hit off either an uphill or downhill lie, simply set the line of your hips and shoulders parallel to the slope you're on. This means adjusting your balance so that most of your weight is on the *lower* foot. For a right-handed player that's the right foot for an uphill lie, the left foot for a downhill lie. Ball position also is important, and you should play it toward the higher foot—the left foot for an uphill lie, the right foot for a downhill lie.

To prevent a fat or topped shot, swing the club along the line of the slope. Starting with the hips and shoulders set parallel to this line

Downslope delofts clubface.

Upslope adds loft to clubface.

Swing the club along the line of the slope.

at address makes this easier.

The steeper the slope, the greater the tendency to lose your balance, so take a few practice swings. You may decide that making a three-quarter swing of the arms, keeping the lower body quiet, will increase your chances of good contact.

The lie and your address posi-

tion influence the shape of the resulting shot. Your setup for an uphill lie naturally adds loft to the clubface, while the angle of the slope also promotes a higher shot. So take a less-lofted club or two, depending on the severity of the hill.

The opposite is true for a downhill lie: Swinging down along the

Flatter swing plane.

More vertical swing plane.

Upright posture

Bend more at waist.

Ball above feet, allow for draw... ball below feet, allow for fade.

slope delofts the clubface, while the angle of the slope creates a lower shot. Go down a club or two.

SIDEHILL

From a sidehill lie, you must alter the swing plane by changing your posture. The lie helps you do this. A ball below your feet forces you to stand closer to it and bend more at the waist, creating a more upright swing plane. A ball above the feet forces you to stand farther away and more erect, encouraging a flatter swing.

In addition to altering the swing plane, sidehill lies also affect the shape of the shot. A ball below the feet forces a very straight take-away with the arms, resulting in an out-to-in approach path and a left-to-right flight pattern. Compensate by aiming a little left, allowing for the fade.

A ball above the feet calls for a great deal of body turn and a flat arm and shoulder plane, resulting in a right-to-left flight. Aim a little right to allow for the draw.

9
SWEEP THE LONG IRONS

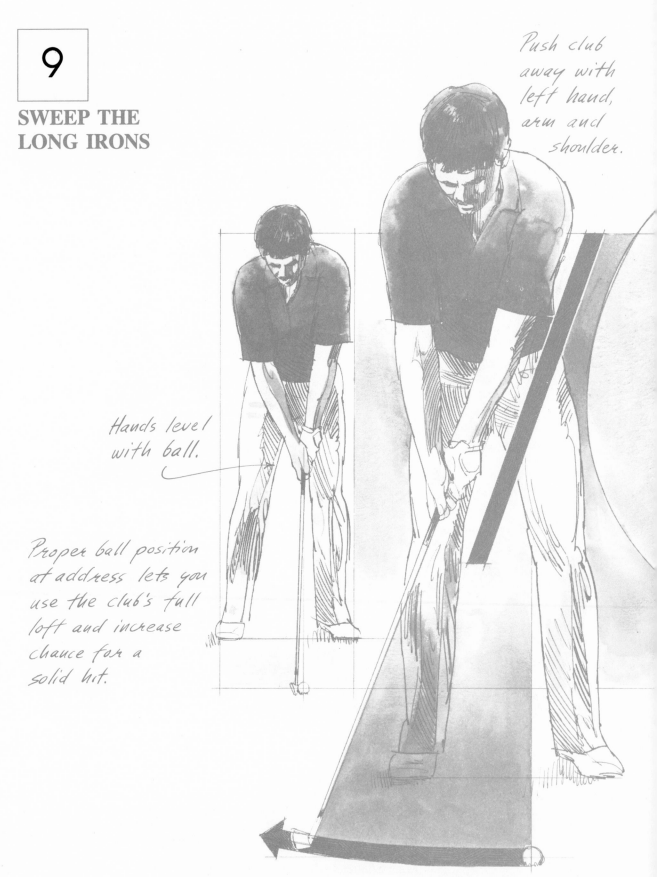

Push club away with left hand, arm and shoulder.

Hands level with ball.

Proper ball position at address lets you use the club's full loft and increase chance for a solid hit.

Keep the club low.

Keep your upper body still and behind ball through impact.

Impact Zone

long iron will send the ball off at a much lower angle.

Set up to the ball to promote a sweeping action through impact. Line up square to your target with the ball opposite the lowest point in your swing. For most players this will be on line with the inside of the left heel. If you play the ball too far back in the stance, you'll make a descending blow, and the clubface will contact the ball with reduced loft. Playing the ball too far forward in your stance runs the risk of topping the shot.

Also, make sure your hands are in line with the ball or just a fraction ahead at address.

PUSH BACK, PULL THROUGH

Your first move away from the ball should establish a low, wide arc. Push the club back with your left hand, arm and shoulder, then strive for a full shoulder turn that forces your weight to shift onto the inside of your right foot. Don't pick up the club with your hands or cock it quickly with your wrists. The wrists will cock naturally at the top of the backswing so you don't have to "make" it happen.

During the downswing, think about keeping your head and upper body still while your weight shifts back to the left and you pull the club smoothly through the ball. Many high handicappers throw their upper body toward the target as a way to get more power. But if your upper body gets ahead of its original address position, the clubface will come into the ball pointing right and with reduced loft. You're probably familiar with the result, a low pushed shot.

The proper setup allows you to utilize the full loft of the club. A good arm swing and shoulder turn keep the club moving in a wide, shallow arc while developing the necessary clubhead speed. And a disciplined downswing around a steady upper body, without lunging, provides solid contact. Work on these keys and increase your confidence with the long irons.

Be honest. How do you feel when you realize you have a long-iron shot to the green? If you break out in a cold sweat, you're not alone. Many high handicappers dread long iron shots: They just don't believe they can hit these clubs.

You'll probably never hit long irons like Greg Norman. But the principles are within everybody's grasp; understanding

them will help you improve greatly.

USE THE LOFT

The 2-iron has about 20 degrees of loft; the 3-iron, 23 or 24 degrees. This is enough to get the ball airborne if the clubhead hits the ball with reasonable speed while traveling on a shallow path. Unless you possess tremendous strength, hitting down with a

10

BEATING THE BURIED LIE

You're right where you don't want to be—in the bunker. If that weren't bad enough, the ball is plugged, most of it below the surface of the soft sand.

Be confident; don't let the situation beat you before you make the shot. You may not be able to knock this shot stiff, but unless the ball's totally buried, you can get it out.

FORGET THE SAND WEDGE
From most bunker shots you'd use a sand wedge, which has a large flange that allows it to skim rather than dig through the sand. But for a buried lie you must dig deeper than normal so that the sand behind the ball pushes it up and out. The sand wedge won't dig deep enough no matter what you do.

Instead, turn to the pitching wedge. Its smaller flange allows the leading edge to dig, and in most cases you can get it under the ball.

FORGET NORMAL TECHNIQUE
From a normal bunker lie, you address the ball with the blade of the sand wedge open to facilitate skimming and add loft to the shot. Also, you swing with an active right side, slapping or slicing through a thin layer of sand so the ball pops up softly and with backspin.

This technique won't work on the buried lie. Here, you must address the ball with the face of the pitching wedge square or even slightly hooded. Keep your stance square with the weight on your left side and the ball centered between your feet.

Aim to hit the sand two inches behind the ball. Use a steep arm swing back and through, keeping

Address with both stance and clubface square, weight left and grip firm.

the weight left. You should feel that the left arm and side are pulling the club down.

The deeper the lie, the more you hood the blade and the harder your swing.

FORGET THE PIN
The ball will fly onto the green in a burst of sand. It will roll a long way after it hits because you can't put backspin on this shot. So, if the pin is cut close to the bunker, forget about getting the ball close. You want to hit the shot with enough force to carry the bank and hit the green. Then let it roll.

With the pin toward the far side of the green, you can get it close simply by letting the ball run to the hole.

You must generate
enough force to
fly the ball to
the green; let it
run from there.

11

MAKE MORE UPHILL AND DOWNHILL PUTTS

Beginners and other high-handicappers run up their scores on the putting green by misjudging uphill and downhill slopes. Very simply, an uphill putt will move more slowly than normal, which means you have to hit it a little firmer. A downhiller will roll more, so you want to hit it softer.

Here are some ways to help you hit putts at different speeds, as well as information on how the slope actually can help you sink more putts.

UPHILL: HIT IT SOLID
Putting straight uphill, the back of the cup is slightly higher than the front. This "backstop" allows you to charge the hole instead of trying to make the ball die over the edge.

Charging the cup makes sense for other reasons, too. First, hitting hard means you don't have to worry as much about pace and break; just aim for the back of the cup and be aggressive. Second, even if you do miss, the slope should keep the ball from running too far past the hole, leaving a short comeback putt.

On an uphill putt, the steeper the slope, the harder you have to strike the ball. It's crucial that you make solid contact, since any distance lost by a mishit will be magnified by the slope. A mis-struck putt that comes up three feet short on a flat surface can end up six feet short when going uphill.

A common fault when trying to hit an aggressive putt is moving the head and body forward during the forward stroke. This sway increases the chances of missing the sweet spot, which will leave a putt well

short. You must keep your body steady on uphill putts.

DOWNHILL: TOPPLE IT IN
On a downhill putt, the back of the cup is *lower* than the front; there's no backstop to save you, so your stroke must be more conservative. Too quick a putt can jump right over the hole.

Aim for the front lip of the cup and try to roll the ball with just enough speed to topple in. You

must judge both the speed and break of the putt almost perfectly, but your chances of holing it are much better than trying to charge the ball through any breaks.

Guard against making a nervous jab that causes the ball to jump and tear down the hill. The slope will magnify your mistakes; a putt that rolls three feet by the hole on a flat surface could end up twice that or more going downhill.

Uphill...back lip is higher.

"Charge" the ball to the cup going uphill.

Downhill...back lip is lower.

Let the ball "die" into the cup going downhill.

Downhill Putting

"Tap The Toe"
To hit a softer putt downhill, address the ball toward the toe of the putter—away from the sweetspot—and strike it there using your normal stroke. You'll get a "dead" impact, preventing the ball from coming off hot and speeding down the hill.

Uphill Putting

"Point Your Chin"
To keep your body still on uphill putts, widen your stance slightly and point your chin straight down at the ball. Your head is probably a little more erect. Keep the chin still and imagine pushing the hands back and pulling them through on a path directly beneath it.

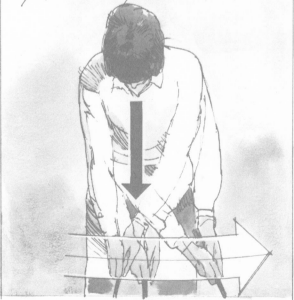

12

A CHECKLIST FOR FAULTS

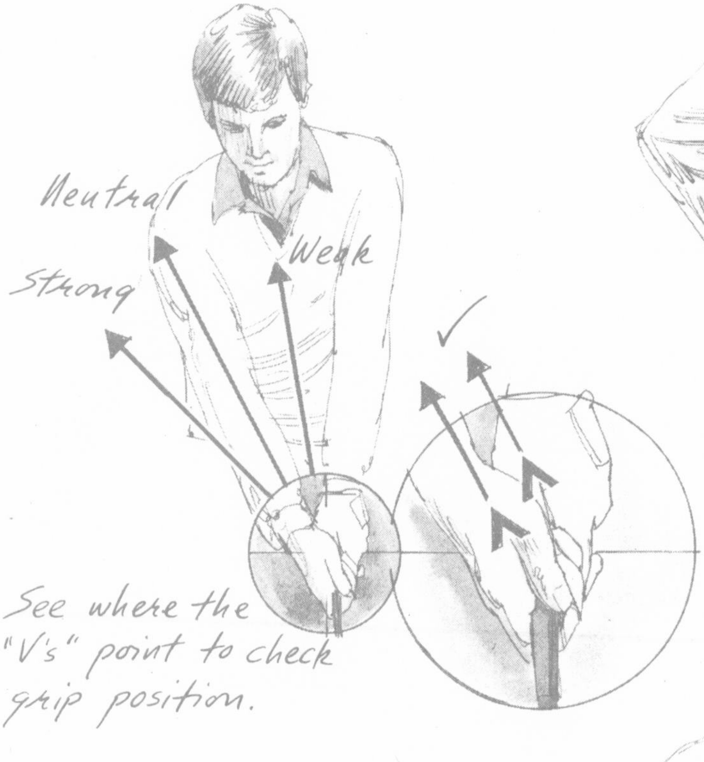

Square

Open

Closed

Neutral

Strong

Weak

See where the "V's" point to check grip position.

Determine your alignment with the help of an extra club.

Lay club along your toes.

Whenever your shots start to sail off line, check your fundamentals first! Most high handicappers look too hard for an exotic fault when their mistakes usually are with their grip, alignment or swing path. Here's what to look for.

THE GRIP

It's easy to spot if you've slipped into too strong or too weak a grip by noting where the Vs formed by the thumb and index finger of each hand are pointing. Vs pointing at the chin indicate a weak grip; at the right shoulder, a neutral grip; past the right shoulder, a strong grip.

A grip that's too weak leaves the clubface open at impact, causing a slice. Too strong closes the clubface, creating a hook. Ideally you want your grip to be neutral. Judging by the shape of your shots, turn the hands to strengthen or weaken the grip and straighten out the ball flight.

ALIGNMENT

To test alignment, pick out a specific target and set up to it in what you think is a square stance. Once you're set, hold that position and lay the club along your toes.

Step away behind the ball and see whether the club points to the target or points to the left (open) or right (closed). An open alignment usually causes a push or slice; a closed stance, a pull or hook. Check the alignment of your hips and shoulders in the same way.

SWING PATH

The easiest way to check your swing path is by observing the basic shape of your shots. A straight ball indicates a good inside-to-inside path. A pull or pull-slice signals an outside-in swing; a push or roundhouse hook, an inside-out swing.

You can get another clue to your swing path by examining the direction and depth of your divots. Hit a few practice shots with a 7-iron. Then "read" the divots: The proper inside-to-inside path produces divots that point slightly left of the target.

An outside-in swing digs divots that are short, deep and point well left of the target. If yours look like this, work on taking the club back on an inside path.

The divot hole of an inside-out swing will be very long, thin and shallow and pointing to the right of the target. To correct this, bring the clubhead back on a straight line away from the ball for the first two feet of the takeaway.

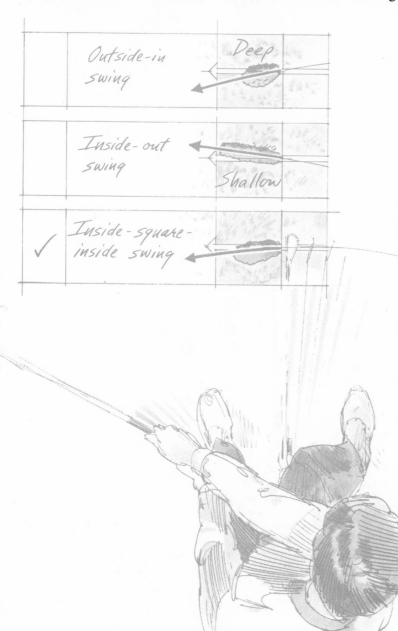

Examining the direction, depth and shape of your divots will help you check your swing path.

13

PLAY YOUR BEST IN A TOURNAMENT

When deciding between two clubs, choose the one you're more confident in.

Before the tournament practice one part of your game that needs sharpening.

On the first tee, take your time and go through your normal pre-shot routine.

It's tournament time at the club and your pals have talked you into playing. Not confident in your skills, you're a little apprehensive and afraid you'll embarrass yourself. Your fears are normal and are shared by many first-timers in organized competition, stroke or match-play. Here are a few tips on how these fears can be overcome.

PRACTICE ONE SHOT

There are probably three or four areas of your game that need sharpening; pick one and concentrate on it before the tournament. Whether it's approach putting, getting out of sand or long irons, devote a little more practice time to it. A little confidence gained in one problem area will boost confidence in your entire game.

KEEP ONE SHOT IN THE BAG

No doubt there is a club or two that you simply don't trust. For example, you're topping the 3-wood from the fairway. So don't risk the possible poor shot—and the blow to your confidence that will come with it. Keep the 3-wood in your bag, hit a club you're sure of, say the 4- or 5-wood, and keep your ego intact.

THE FIRST TEE IS THE WORST TEE

The opening drive usually sets the tone for the rest of the round. Smack one down the middle and the butterflies in your stomach disappear; top it and they multiply.

On the first tee, take your time and go through your normal pre-shot routine. Don't rush. Relax. Focus on head position and tempo: Keep your head still and swing smoothly and you'll make good contact.

The real opponent is the course.

Look at your first tournament as a learning experience.

CLASH WITH THE COURSE

You probably will be grouped with players of similar skills who are just as nervous as you are. Instead of competing against them, play against the course. Although you'll never find a more unfaltering opponent, if you play well against the course, you're almost guaranteed to do well in the standings.

LEARN TO HANDLE PRESSURE

Ever wonder how a Tour pro can appear calm stepping up to the potential winning putt? Most will admit they were nervous but had learned to control their nerves by having been in similar situations before. They actually have had practice at being under pressure.

You can do the same, to a cer-

tain degree, by using your imagination during practice. Chip balls onto the practice green pretending you need an up-and-down to win. Hit tee shots on the driving range imagining you're on 18 needing par for victory, so it's crucial that you hit the fairway. Putt four footers at home pretending each one will win you the U.S. Open.

But the best practice of all is the tournament itself. Your first competitive experience is a learning experience, and it's no disgrace to lose. Tour pros believe you can learn how to win—but first you must learn how to lose.

14

YOU CAN KEEP YOUR HEAD DOWN

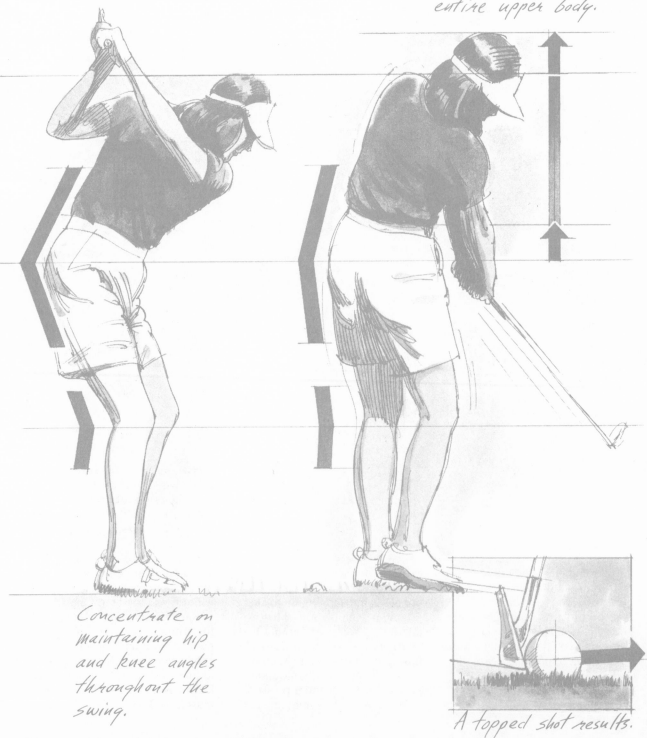

If you straighten up at the waist or straighten your legs, you will raise your entire upper body.

Concentrate on maintaining hip and knee angles throughout the swing.

A topped shot results.

Just as annoying as a bad shot is the sound of a playing partner blurting, "You lifted your head!"

Although your helpful friend may, indeed, have seen your head rise, the problem really is too much body movement. Most instruction calls for keeping the head down or still, because doing so keeps the body quiet throughout the swing. Some players become so intent on keeping their heads still that they tense their upper bodies—restricting the turn—and ignore parts of the body they should be concentrating on, the angle between the spine and hips and the flex of the knees.

Straightening either of these angles during the swing results in lifting the head and also raises the arc of the swing so the clubhead contacts the top of the ball.

Conversely, bending more at either the knees or hips during the swing drops the head and upper body and lowers the arc of the swing so the club strikes too far behind the ball, usually into the ground.

So forget your head and concentrate on maintaining the angles at the hips and knees from address through impact. Then you shouldn't be bothered again by topped or fat shots.

Shadow Drill

For this drill, you'll need a source of light behind you to cast your shadow directly in front of you at address. Position yourself so you can see the top of your shadow's head. Mark a line there and practice swinging. If you're "keeping your head down," your shadow's head will stay relatively even with the line. If not, practice until it does.

WEDGE WORK

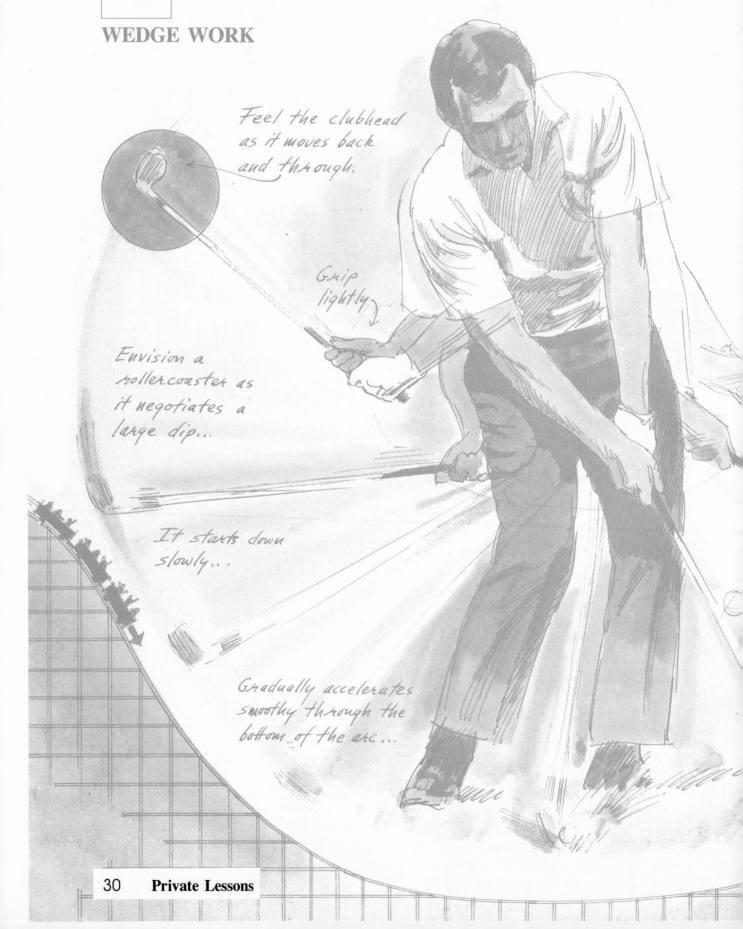

Feel the clubhead as it moves back and through.

Grip lightly

Envision a rollercoaster as it negotiates a large dip...

It starts down slowly...

Gradually accelerates smoothly through the bottom of the arc...

High handicappers who could lower their score by sharpening their short-game technique too often are scared of the wedges. Laying the blade of a pitching or sand wedge behind the ball conjures up thoughts of chili-dips, skulled shots and worse. In rushing to get the shot over, they rush the swing as well, virtually guaranteeing a poor shot.

If wedges scare you, here's a three-step process to simplify your short game and start bringing down your scores.

1. KEEP THINGS SIMPLE
You've probably seen pros on television opening their stance, laying the club wide open and making other changes in technique to hit finesse shots. But you should stop experimenting and go with the basics. Keep things as simple as possible by using your normal grip and a square clubface. Open your stance only slightly. After you start making consistently crisp contact you can experiment with stance, grip and clubface alignment to play different shots.

2. HIT DOWN FOR UP
Beginners commonly try to scoop the ball in the air by exaggerating hand action. The ball doesn't need help—that's the reason the clubface is angled. To let the club do its job, you have to hit down on the ball.

Force yourself to hit down by imagining a small wedge of wood behind the ball. Aim to drive the wedge under the ball with the leading edge of the club, and you'll get the ball airborne while eliminating blades and skulls.

3. SLOW AND SMOOTH
A major cause of mishit wedge shots is excessive body movement, usually caused by swinging too quickly. If the body lifts during the downswing, the clubhead hits high on the ball, causing a bladed or skulled shot. If the body drops, the club hits behind the ball for a fat shot. A hurried downswing also may cause coming over the top and pulling the ball left.

Think of the wedge as a precision instrument used to hit the ball an exact distance and direction. The wedge should be handled lightly, with deftness and finesse, not heavy-handedly. Hold the grip lightly and take half-swings without thinking about mechanics. Concentrate solely on feeling the rhythm of the clubhead back and through. Envision a rollercoaster as it negotiates a large dip: Starting downhill slowly, it gradually picks up speed and accelerates through the bottom arc, gradually slowing as it climbs the next hill. Forget about the ball and try only to swing the clubhead with that same rhythm.

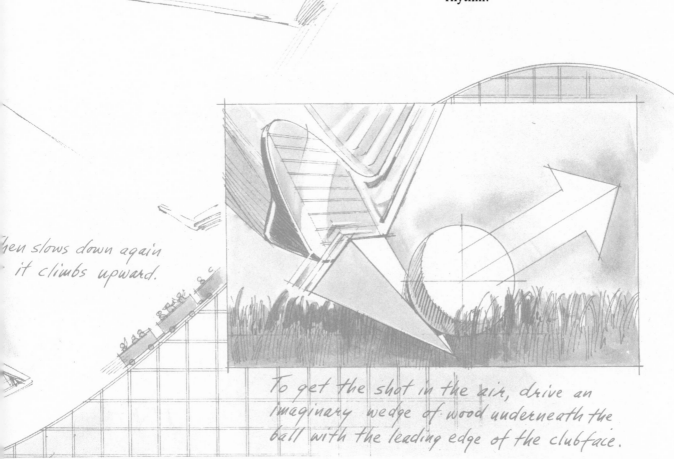

then slows down again it climbs upward.

To get the shot in the air, drive an imaginary wedge of wood underneath the ball with the leading edge of the clubface.

16

ALLOW FOR THE WIND

There's an old Scottish expression, "If there's nae wind, it's nae golf." A variety of wind conditions and a breeze make a big difference in how to play any shot. A strong wind at your back, for example, can help you hit the green of a par five in two shots; the same wind in the face might make three shots almost impossible.

To score your best, you must respect and understand the wind's effect on the ball. Here are the basics.

HEADWINDS

The toughest wind is the one that blows directly into your face.

A stiff breeze can have a big effect on distance and ball flight.

Tailwind decreases amount of curve.

Headwind incre amount of curve

Knowing that you'll lose some distance, usually you swing harder, which compounds the wind's effects by creating a bad shot.

Instead of letting the wind beat you psychologically, determine how much distance you're giving up, take enough extra club and concentrate on making solid contact. Don't be shy about taking enough stick. A good rule of thumb is to add one club for about every 10 miles per hour of wind. For example, if you're looking straight into a 30 mph gale, take three more clubs; if the shot is a 7-iron in no wind, hit a 4-iron. Be sure to make a smooth swing.

A headwind also magnifies the curve of a slice or fade, so be sure to allow for it. The stronger the wind, the greater effect on your shot. A right-to-left hook or draw travels on a lower trajectory, so its flight is less affected by headwind.

TAILWINDS

Teeing off with a wind behind you would seem to be ideal: The ball will stay in the air longer for more distance. But a following wind will bring the ball down on a shallower angle than normal, so it will come in "hot" and roll more than usual.

CROSSWINDS

There are two methods for handling a crosswind: Either work the ball into the wind, e.g. hit a left-to-right shot into a right-to-left breeze, or let the wind do the work. The latter method is easier.

Plan on the ball shifting approximately five yards for every 10 miles per hour of wind speed. For example, aim about 10 yards left of your target when hitting through a 20 mph, left-to-right crosswind.

Remember that a crosswind will effect the shape of the shot, which should have some bearing on your aim. Depending on the direction of the wind, it will either increase or decrease the amount of bend on a fade or draw.

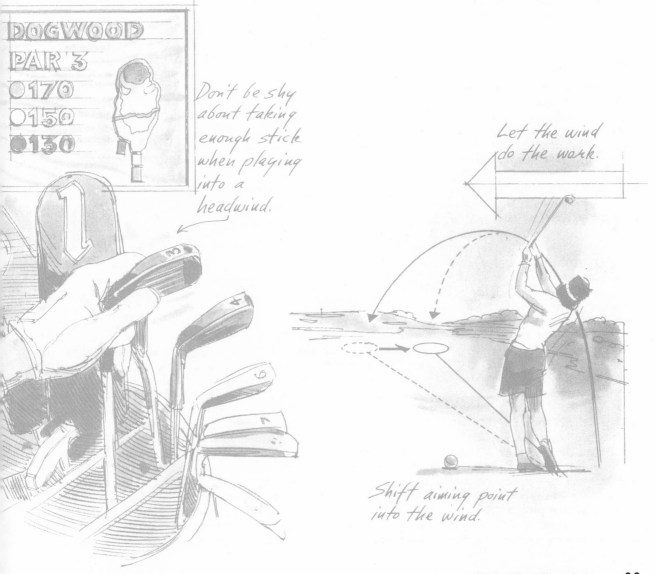

17

GROOVE AN INSIDE PATH

The slice is the bane of nearly all high handicappers. Even when you make what feels like your best contact, the ball flies with a high, lazy drift from left to right, costing you yards and accuracy.

If you slice, your clubhead is traveling from outside to inside the target line. To correct it, you must ingrain a swinging action in which the clubhead *never* moves outside the target line—it only moves *onto* the target line as it contacts the ball. You need to groove an "inside" swing path.

MOVE CLUB BACK WITH BODY, NOT HANDS

Most high handicappers lift the club back with their arms. The club may not move outside the actual target line, but it does move outside the path it should take when it revolves around the body in an "on-plane" position.

To start back on-plane, try this: Instead of moving the club back with your arms, turn your upper body and your arms away from the ball together. This way, the body turn establishes a consistent takeaway path, instead of a random, hands-oriented movement.

Of course, your body must be aligned parallel to the target line, with your upper body bent slightly toward the ball.

TURN BACK TO TARGET

Many golfers measure the completeness of their backswing by the position of the clubshaft at the top. You may think that if the clubshaft has reached horizontal, you've made a complete backswing. But you've probably gotten the club back by breaking your left arm and cocking your wrists, not by turning the body around your spine.

Strive for as full a body turn as you can, so that your arms and

The clubhead comes back gradually inside the target line, responding to body turn.

the clubhead stay on the plane established by your shoulder turn. If you do this, the clubhead will move on a smooth plane coming gradually inside the target line.

UNCOIL DOWN SAME PATH

Making a full body coil going back makes it easier to groove an inside path on the downswing. You'll automatically start down along the same path that brought the club back by releasing the pent-up energy stored in the backswing.

When you make a lazy backswing turn using your arms only, there's little energy stored at the top. Invariably, you'll move your hands and arms to the outside as the "hit impulse" takes over and you chop at the ball in a steeply-descending, outside-in fashion.

Work on an improved backswing turn in which your arms follow the full coiling of your torso. Really work to build that instant of tension at the top. Then you can let the downswing uncoil along the same inside path you swung back on.

Back
faces
target.

Full body turn
establishes an
on-plane backswing,
proper downswing.

SAND TEXTURES

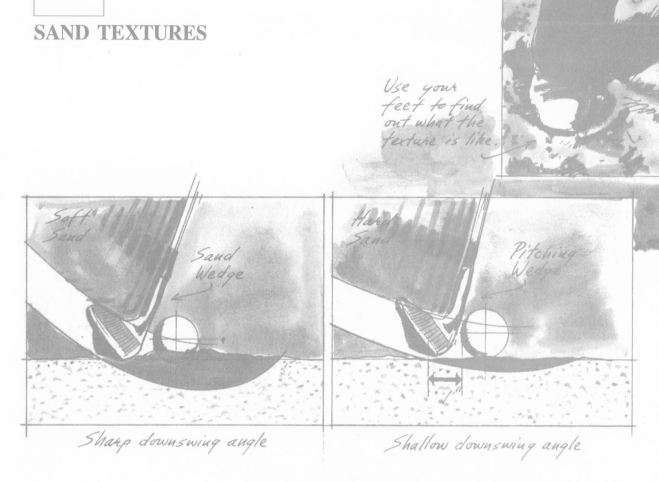

Use your feet to find out what the texture is like.

Soft Sand — *Sand Wedge* — *Sharp downswing angle*

Hard Sand — *Pitching Wedge* — *Shallow downswing angle*

Sand traps bother all golfers, so there's no reason high handicappers should be any different. One reason for their fear is the skulled escape shot that sails over the green, often into another trap. To cure this ugly shot, you first must understand how different textures of sand affect your play.

Although designed primarily for bunker play, the sand wedge is not always the right club to use from a trap. Its wide, rounded flange makes the club bounce through dry, fine sand, throwing a thin layer—and the ball—into the air. But sand isn't always soft and fluffy. Wet sand is heavy and tends to stick together, and if you're playing after a hard rain, the surface probably will be packed down and as hard as a car path.

As if that weren't enough, not all dry sand is soft and grainy. The sand on some courses is simply rougher and coarser than on others. Like everything else in golf, you have to know what affect this variety of conditions will have on your shotmaking and plan accordingly.

FIRM SAND: USE A PITCHING WEDGE

For a greenside shot from firm sand, trade your sand club for a pitching wedge. Its sharper face and smaller flange dig in and under the ball better than the sand wedge, which would bounce off the hard surface and skull the ball. But don't let the blade of the pitching wedge dig in too deeply. Set up a little wider than usual and make a low, sweeping takeaway and hit down briskly about an inch behind the ball to "skim" it out.

If the sand is hard-packed so even the sharp edge of your pitching wedge will bounce up and "belly" the ball, play the shot as you would off hard dirt. Square the blade, play it back in your stance, set the hands ahead and pick the ball cleanly off the surface.

TEST WITH YOUR FEET

Use your feet to test the texture. For example, make sure that what you think is packed sand isn't really a thin crust with fluffy sand underneath. If it is, take the sand wedge and play a normal explosion shot.

Hit briskly about an inch behind the ball and "skin" it out.

Set up a little wider, and make a low, sweeping takeaway.

19

SHAKE THE SHANKS

The ball is struck with the hosel of the club.

Keep the head back throughout the swing.

Hands ahead of the ball.

Set weight more toward your heels.

Dowel Stick Drill

You can firm up your hand action and shake the shanks with the help of a friend, a wooden dowel about a foot-and-a-half long and a few plastic practice balls. Holding a wedge, set up with your hands ahead of the ball; have your friend touch the back of your left hand with the stick. Have him hold the stick in that position as you swing. On the downswing, concentrate on the left hand hitting the stick at the same time the clubhead hits the ball.

The worst shot in golf has to be the shank, a mishit that squirts to the right almost perpendicular to your target line. The shank is caused by the ball being struck by the hosel of the club instead of the clubface.

There are three main causes of shanking: Setting up with too much weight toward the toes (and keeping it there as you swing); moving the head during the swing; and sloppy hand and wrist action through impact. What follows are ways to counter each problem.

DISTRIBUTE YOUR WEIGHT EQUALLY
Placing your weight too much toward the toes or heels during the setup and the swing causes you to lose balance in the downswing. If you fall forward coming down, the position of the swing plane changes, and the club hits the ball off the hosel.

Distribute your weight equally between the ball and heel of each foot. Try adding a little more knee flex—that naturally shifts more weight toward the heels.

KEEP YOUR HEAD STILL
This really is a way to keep the upper body from lunging toward the ball on the downswing. You want to swing with the arms, but if the upper body takes over and moves toward the ball, the plane of the swing changes and the club comes into the ball hosel-first. As the body lunges, the head moves too, so concentrate on keeping the head still to quiet the action.

Imagine that at address your head is resting lightly against a pane of glass. Concentrate on swinging down with the hands and arms while keeping your head behind the glass; if you "break the glass," you are lunging at the ball. Keeping the head back will keep your body from moving and allow you to return the clubface squarely to the ball.

FIRM UP THE HANDS AND WRISTS
The hands should be slightly ahead of the clubhead at the moment of impact. But should the left wrist break down in the downswing, the clubhead will be cast ahead of the hands, often causing a shanked shot.

To keep the left wrist from breaking, firm up the tension in your left hand and wrist and start with your hands slightly ahead of the ball. On the takeaway, push the club straight back, keeping the left arm firm (but not overly stiff) until the wrists start to cock naturally. Your goal is to make the position of the hands at impact be the same as they started at address.

20

HANDLING THE BIG BREAKERS

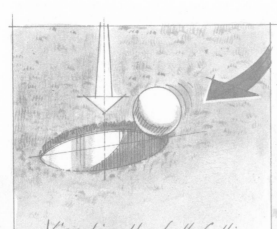

Visualize the ball falling in the side door instead of the front edge.

Learn to trust the break by gradually aiming farther and farther away from the cup.

Every so often you play a course with heavily contoured greens. Big contours make for big breaks, which can lead to three putts if you don't negotiate them properly. Not allowing for enough break on a putt that swings from five to 10 feet to either side could mean you face a five to 10 footer on your second putt. Here's how to tame the big breaks.

TRUST THE BREAK

Many golfers leave the ball well below the hole on big breaks because they can't bring themselves to aim too far away from the cup. This is especially true on short putts with a lot of movement.

To get more comfortable with aiming way off the cup, you must practice and convince yourself that the ball really will move.

Find a putt of about 15 feet with a lot of break. Make your first putt aiming directly at the cup; note how far it falls from the cup. Putt four more balls, aiming a little farther from the cup each time. The ball should finish closer and closer to the hole. Eventually you will reach a point where you're aiming well away from the cup yet the contour is bringing the ball back to it.

THINK SIDE DOOR

Most golfers zero in on the front or back of the cup when lining up a putt. But for putts with big breaks, try visualizing the ball falling in a side door. This image will help you get comfortable with the idea of aiming the ball far from the hole and allow you to hit it high enough to have a chance of finding the cup.

Drill:

Roll It Around The Shaft

One way to get used to aiming away from the hole on a big breaking putt is to give yourself an obstacle to get around. Find a putt with a big swing and lay a golf club down on an angle in front of the hole, forcing you to use the break to get the ball around the shaft and to the cup.

USE DIFFERENT CLUBS FOR CHIPPING

Your shoulder, arm and wrist movement should resemble your putting stroke.

Very narrow, open stance

Use a more lofted club as you move farther from the green's surface.

Which club do you grab when your ball is sitting just off the green? Do you always chip with the same one? Using the same club from a variety of distances off the green has a big drawback: You have to change the force of your stroke from soft for short chips to hard for long ones. A more reliable way to get the ball up and down is by varying the club rather than the force of the stroke.

Think of the chip shot as a long approach putt, the main objective being to get the ball on the green as soon as possible and running it up to the hole. If the ball rests a few feet from the surface—so there's little fringe to fly over—a low-lofted club such as a 4- or 5-iron will do the trick. Use a more lofted club as you move farther from the green. Using different clubs lets you make the same stroke, with little variation in force, for more consistent results.

The chipping motion should resemble your putting stroke in the amount of arm, shoulder and wrist movement. The one significant difference is the stance: Set up narrow and open for the chip, with the ball centered between the feet and your hands even with or slightly ahead of it. For crisp contact, keep your hands ahead of the clubhead through impact.■

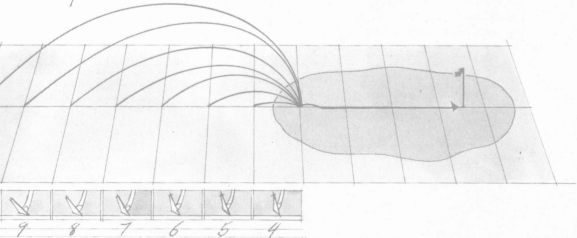

Power Hitter

You hit the ball a long way, but rarely as straight as you want. Your game needs control and consistency.

Nothing excites the golfer like the long ball, and this is the guy who can hit it. But prodigious power often is disastrous. The shot that would drift just a little right or left off someone else's club becomes a monstrous miss thanks to the enormous clubhead speed generated by the big hitter. So while the ball may be 280 yards down-range, it's also 50 yards off-line.

The power hitter's biggest enemy is himself. Until he can learn to control his swing—keeping it compact, smooth, and under control—he's going to play courses from the sides. That's why this chapter deals primarily with tempering the big swing. But throttling back won't happen overnight, and until then, the power hitter will find trouble. So many of the lessons offer help navigating from trees, sand, rough, mud, and other unnatural habitats.

Finally, although the power hitter needs to bring his big swing under control, he shouldn't become a powder puff. Sometimes the gorilla should unleash what he's got, whether to gain a strategic advantage or execute an otherwise impossible shot. Like a supercharged sports car, the power hitter can't run all-out all the time, but those horses under the hood are sure to come in handy.

1

MAKE A THREE-QUARTER SWING

You rarely hit two solid, straight shots back-to-back. That long, loose action you've developed sends the ball off wildly, costing you penalties as well as shots wasted getting back into play.

You should be ready to sacrifice a bit of distance to become a far more consistent player. It's time to adopt the three-quarter swing. Here's how.

TAKE A WIDER STANCE

You need to develop a tight coiling pattern on the backswing and reduce any tendency to sway—as most wild hitters do. Take a wider-than-normal stance, so your legs become a stable base for your arm swing and shoulder turn.

With a driver, take a stance slightly wider than shoulder width. Position the ball no farther forward in your stance than the left heel. Many power hitters play the ball too far forward, off the left toe, so they have to lunge to reach the ball. Instead, you should feel nicely centered over the ball at address.

For shorter clubs, your stance will narrow progressively, but keep it two to three inches wider than you ordinarily would.

LEAVE ROOM AT THE TOP

Swing the club back without any conscious effort to break your wrists. They'll hinge naturally as you approach the top. You'll feel your weight shifting onto your right foot, but make sure that it stays on the *inside* of that foot—if it goes outside, you're swaying.

Most power hitters take the driver back at least to horizontal, some well beyond. Even if you think you can swing back much further, take the driver back only to the three-quarter position—midway between perpendicular and parallel to the ground.

The three-quarter swing:

1) Helps keep your weight on

Stance for the driver is wider than the shoulders.

Ball positioned just inside left heel.

the inside of your right foot, reducing any sway.

2) Limits wrist action—opening or closing the clubface at the top—which must be compensated for on the downswing.

3) Reduces the chance of losing the proper clubshaft position at the top (pointing at the target rather than left or right of it).

TIME YOUR DOWNSWING

From the three-quarter position, swing down keying on two funda-

mentals—shifting your weight onto your left foot and pulling the club through impact to a full follow-through.

Don't worry if your timing feels a bit off at first and you feel the urge to overpower the ball. Stick with it. You'll soon be striking the ball more squarely and at least as far as before because your swing is more compact. But best of all, your distance will be much more *consistent*—because you'll have fewer off-center hits.

Keep wrists firm
and swing back to a
point where shaft is
halfway between
perpendicular and
parallel to the
ground.

2

TREE SURVIVAL GUIDE

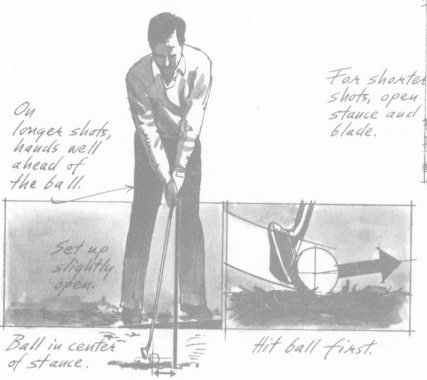

On longer shots, hands well ahead of the ball.

Set up slightly open.

Ball in center of stance.

Hit ball first.

For shorter shots, open stance and blade.

Explode the ball.

Well, there you are again: 280 yards off the tee but so deep in the woods that you'd like to trade your 5-iron for a power saw. How should you play it—gamble or get safely back in the fairway?

PLAY IT SAFE!
If you're in the trees, get back to the fairway. Power players too often look toward the green, pick out an opening between the trunks and hope to steer a shot through and onto the putting surface. That's the ultimate low-percentage shot, more likely to ricochet even deeper into the woods.

Instead, realize that a bogey isn't a bad price to pay for an errant tee shot. Then find the safest way back to the fairway, even if it means pitching out sideways. You

still can hit the green with your next shot and one-putt for par.

PLAYING OFF PINE NEEDLES
Wherever pine trees grow, pine needles fall, presenting a challenge to the golfer who has to play off them.

For long shots off pine needles, play the ball as you would from a fairway bunker: slightly open stance; ball midway between the feet; hands well ahead. Take care not to ground the club, which might cause the ball to move, giving you a one-shot penalty. Make a low takeaway and a sweeping downswing, making sure to hit the ball first.

For shorter shots off needles, rather than trying to pick the ball

clean, explode the way you would from sand. This is especially wise when the bed of needles is thick and spongy.

For the explosion, take an open stance, open the blade and hit about an inch behind the ball. Keep the wrists firm and the clubface open while concentrating on sliding it underneath the ball. Use the pitching wedge; its sharper edge will more easily cut through the needles. The shot will land with almost no spin, so allow for it to roll.

RESTRICTED BACKSWING
Sometimes a tree trunk or branch restricts the backswing. Oftentimes it distracts you to the point of hitting a poor shot.

Most players approach the shot

For a restricted swing, measure the backswing carefully.

Hit about an inch behind.

The "No-Backswing" Swing Drill

If you get rattled when your backswing is restricted, try this drill. Address the ball and set the club in a ½ to ¾ backswing position. Freeze the swing in that spot, the wrists cocked and weight on your right side. Hit practice shots from this position, taking care to shift your weight left and hit down with the arms and hands. On the course, when you encounter a restricted backswing, set the club as far back as you can, then hit the ball.

by making several practice swings, getting a feel for how far back they can take the club. But when it's time to hit the ball, they tense up, make a fast backswing and bang the club into the obstruction, almost always ruining the shot.

When you have a restricted backswing, take some practice swings to get the feel for length. Make a special effort to take the club back slowly and deliberately. The function of the backswing is to set the club in position for the downswing, so a slower-than-usual action won't hurt you.

Bring the club back slowly, even allowing it to tap the trunk or branch at the top, then swing down crisply with the arms and hands, keeping your head still to ensure square contact.

3

SET UP SQUARE

Approach ball from rear.

When you set up square, your shoulders, hips and feet are aligned parallel to the target line.

Imagine standing on a set of railroad tracks that run straight to your target.

The key to any "target" sport—archery, target shooting, bowling or golf—is aim. You must properly aim your body, but it can be difficult to tell when you're right on or far off. Even a subtle deviation from a "square" position can have dire effects on the direction of your shots.

A common misconception in golf is that you have to be aimed right at the target. Because you stand to the side of the ball, not

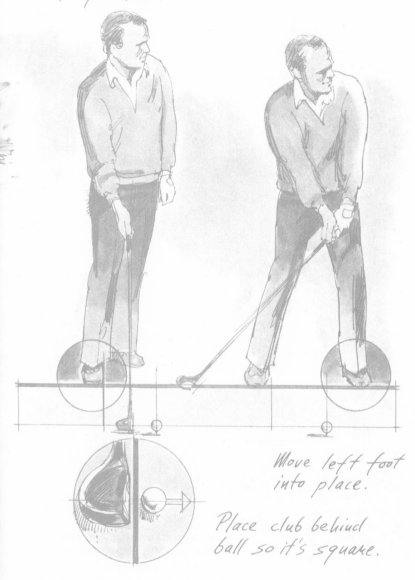

Position right instep perpendicular to target line.

Move left foot into place.

Place club behind ball so it's square.

Intentionally setting up open or closed can help you maneuver the ball, hitting a fade or draw when the shot demands it. But for now, you should be happy to land the ball in the fairway or on the green. Your best bet is to keep things simple and set up square. If you're aligned square to the target line, a reasonably good swing will produce a reasonably straight shot. You probably won't hit the ball dead straight; instead, a hook or draw will result, depending on your timing and hand action, but keeping the ball's movement to a minimum gives it the best chance of landing near the target.

Setting up square requires more than simply aiming your feet parallel to the target line. Your hips and shoulders also must be square. Having them open at address almost guarantees cutting across the ball for a left-to-right shot; closing them produces right-to-left spin.

Another hint is to set up with the right shoulder a little lower than the left. This puts your hands slightly ahead of the ball, promoting the proper angle of attack for the club, while allowing an extra split-second for the clubface to roll into the proper position at impact.

Here is a preaddress checklist to help you set up square:

1) Approach the ball from directly behind, imagining a line running from the ball to your target, the target line;

2) Place your right foot perpendicular to the target line;

3) Position the club behind the ball so the face points at the target;

4) Move your left foot into place perpendicular to the target line, parallel to the right foot;

5) Make sure your hips and shoulders are square with the line established by your feet;

6) Point your left toe slightly toward the target;

7) Waggle a few times to loosen up and get comfortable, but take care not to waggle into an open or closed alignment.

directly behind it, when you swing, you actually should be lined up *parallel* to a line running from the ball to the flag or your landing spot in the fairway. Imagine you are standing on one rail of a railroad track and the ball is on the other; your body should be aligned parallel to the track that runs from the ball to the target.

If your body is pointing at the target (and you play right-handed), you are setting up closed to the target line: Your feet, hips and shoulders are pointing to the right and the club will travel on an inside-out path in relation to the line. What results is either a hook (if the clubface is square to the target at impact) or a pushed shot (if the face is open).

An open stance, pointing left of the line, results in an outside-in swing path, which causes a slice (if the clubface is square) or a pull (if it is closed).

4

THE FEARSOME FLYER

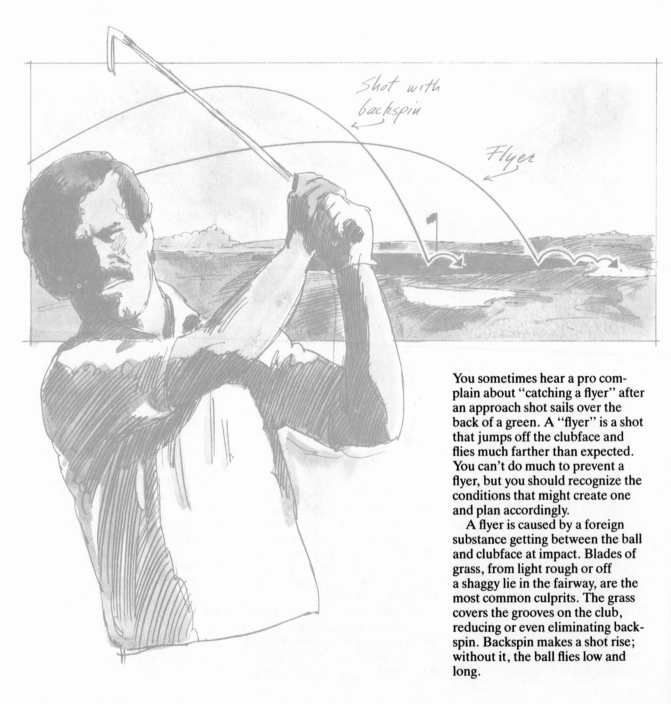

Shot with backspin

Flyer

You sometimes hear a pro complain about "catching a flyer" after an approach shot sails over the back of a green. A "flyer" is a shot that jumps off the clubface and flies much farther than expected. You can't do much to prevent a flyer, but you should recognize the conditions that might create one and plan accordingly.

A flyer is caused by a foreign substance getting between the ball and clubface at impact. Blades of grass, from light rough or off a shaggy lie in the fairway, are the most common culprits. The grass covers the grooves on the club, reducing or even eliminating backspin. Backspin makes a shot rise; without it, the ball flies low and long.

A flyer can be caused by blades of grass coming between the ball and club.

Wet conditions also can produce a flyer, especially with long irons. The sweeping swing path required to hit a long iron causes the clubface to pick up moisture from the grass as it approaches the ball. The water fills the grooves of the clubface, preventing them from doing their job. So watch for flyers out of wet rough or off a wet fairway.

Not only does a flyer sail through the air, it continues rolling after landing. Again, the lack of backspin is the reason. With backspin, a ball bites and stops on a green; without it, the ball lands and keeps running.

There's not much you can do when facing a flyer lie. But if a flyer looks likely, allow for it: Since you know the ball will fly lower, farther and land hot, you might take one less club on approach shots. You may even take two clubs less if trouble lurks behind the green.

Wet conditions can also produce a flyer.

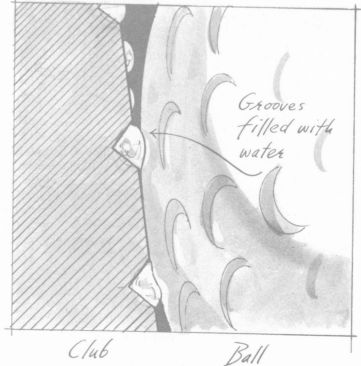

Grooves filled with water

Club

Ball

5

THREE SOFT SHOTS

Break wrists early.

Slightly open stance.

Choke down and make a slow three quarter swing.

1. Low, Controlled Driver

Don't allow hands to release through ball.

Keep left heel flat on ground.

You long hitters not only hit tee shots with power, you hit *every* shot with power. Sooner or later, however, you'll face a shot that shouldn't be muscled; in fact, using force would be detrimental. It's about time you learned some "soft shots," not short game, but finesse play that will make you a more complete golfer.

THE LOW, CONTROLLED DRIVER

Most tight par fours require the 3-wood or less for control. But into the wind the shot needs to be low as well. Take your driver and choke down about an inch. Tee the ball at normal height, play it off your left heel and make a slow three-quarter backswing, keeping your left heel flat on the ground. On the downswing, allow your hips and legs to turn fully through the shot, but don't release your hands. Concentrate instead on holding onto the club as the lower body pulls the arms through impact. The result will be a safe, low shot with a left-to-right

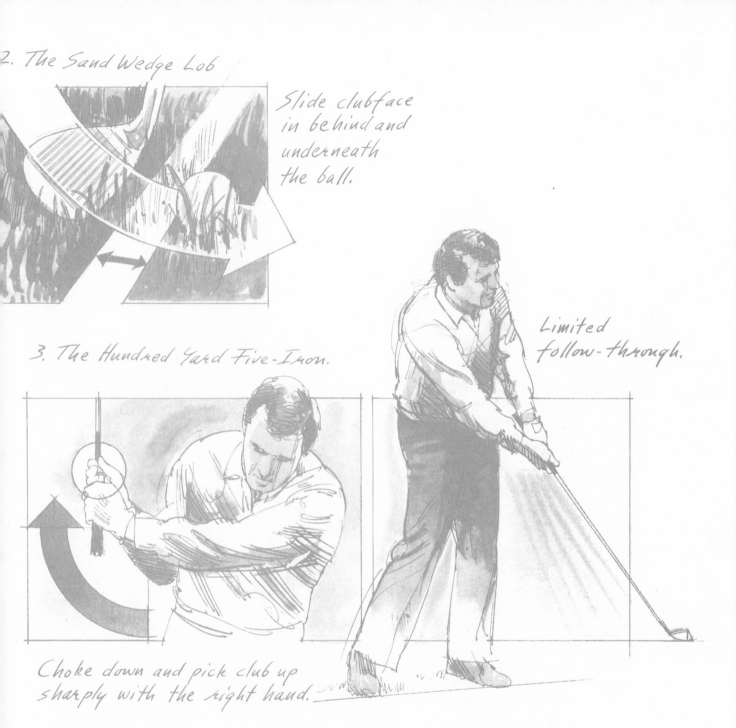

2. The Sand Wedge Lob

Slide clubface in behind and underneath the ball.

3. The Hundred Yard Five-Iron.

Limited follow-through.

Choke down and pick club up sharply with the right hand.

trajectory that flies under the wind and lands with roll.

THE SAND WEDGE LOB
When your ball comes to rest in deep greenside rough and you have little green to work with, put away the pitching wedge and lob it out with the sand wedge.

Address the ball with a slightly open stance and open clubface, the way you would an explosion shot from a bunker. Make a long, slow backswing, breaking the wrists early. Swing down slowly, as though you're pitching a horseshoe, keeping the motion steady—don't decelerate. Slide the clubface in about an inch behind the ball, making an effort to follow through. It will pop out high, with little spin, and land softly.

THE 100-YARD 5-IRON
Although you're probably proud of your long, high short irons, it's time you traded in this shot for a low-flyer that will help you score well when an errant tee shot leaves you under a tree or you want to keep out of the wind or firm greens make running the ball to the pin a better option. That's where it's handy to know how to play the 100-yard 5-iron.

Choke down just short of the metal. Pick the club up sharply with the right hand on the backswing and strike the ball with a steep downswing path and limited follow-through. If you want the ball to land "hot" and roll a long way, hood the blade; for a shot that takes a couple of skips and stops, open the blade.

6

MAKE A SMOOTH TRANSITION

Concentrate on getting the club to the top using your legs, back and shoulders.

A crucial juncture in the swing is the change of direction between the end of the backswing and the start of the downswing. If the transition is smooth and controlled, chances are the downswing will click and the shot will be straight. A fast, jerky change of direction at the top almost invariably leads to a poor downswing and a mishit or misdirected shot.

START WITH A SMOOTH BACKSWING

You don't hit the ball with your backswing, so it doesn't make sense to swing back fast. The backswing sets the body in a coiled position, storing energy for the downswing, and the hands, arms and club in the right places to promote a good downswing path.

The position at the top of the backswing is similar to that of a baseball batter at the plate—he doesn't make a backswing; he starts from the "top."

To slow down a fast backswing, concentrate on getting the club to the top using your legs, back and shoulder muscles—not arms and hands. Bring the club back to a slow, controlled stop at the top, not a hard, abrupt halt. It may help to incorporate a split-second pause before starting the downswing. When you do begin to swing down, always initiate the action with the lower body.

Visualize your hands coasting to a smooth, controlled stop and pausing for a split-second.

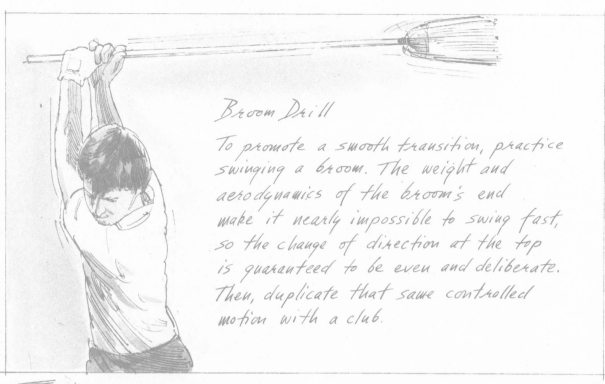

Broom Drill

To promote a smooth transition, practice swinging a broom. The weight and aerodynamics of the broom's end make it nearly impossible to swing fast, so the change of direction at the top is guaranteed to be even and deliberate. Then, duplicate that same controlled motion with a club.

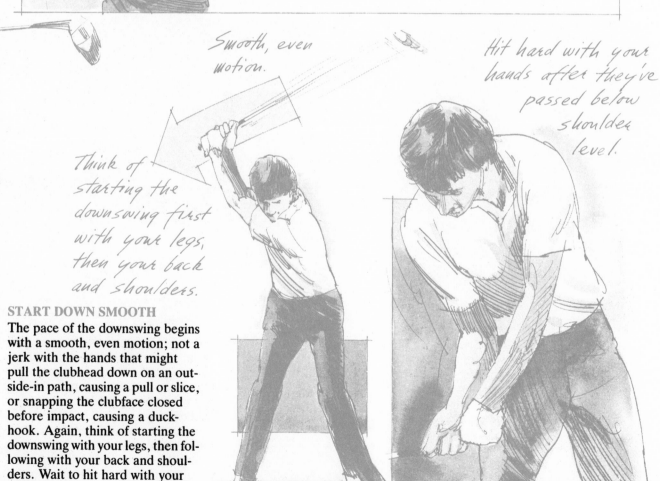

Smooth, even motion.

Think of starting the downswing first with your legs, then your back and shoulders.

Hit hard with your hands after they've passed below shoulder level.

START DOWN SMOOTH

The pace of the downswing begins with a smooth, even motion; not a jerk with the hands that might pull the clubhead down on an outside-in path, causing a pull or slice, or snapping the clubface closed before impact, causing a duckhook. Again, think of starting the downswing with your legs, then following with your back and shoulders. Wait to hit hard with your hands until they've passed below shoulder level, then go ahead and release them.

7

FROM FAIRWAY SAND

Three-quarter arm swing

Play the ball back about a ball width.

Missing fairways usually means finding some kind of trouble, usually rough, sand, woods or water. One of the most frustrating trouble spots is a fairway bunker. Learning how to get the ball out will let you avoid needless headaches and wasted strokes.

Start by choosing a club with enough loft to fly the ball over the lip of the trap. Sometimes a high lip will force you to play a club

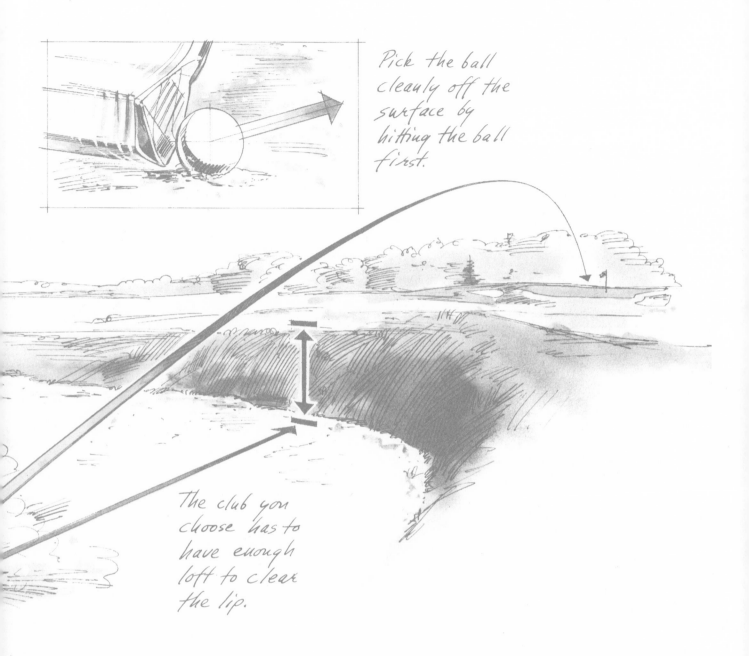

Pick the ball cleanly off the surface by hitting the ball first.

The club you choose has to have enough loft to clear the lip.

that won't get the ball to the target. In that situation, your priority is to get safely out and back into the fairway.

CLEAN CONTACT
For short sand shots from greenside bunkers, the usual procedure is to blast the ball out by hitting into the sand behind it. The clubhead never touches the ball but hits the sand, which propels the ball up and out with it.

From a fairway trap, however, the object is distance. You want to hit the ball first, picking it cleanly off the surface. Catching any sand before contact will slow the club, deadening the force of impact and reducing distance: the more sand, the less distance.

To help you pick it clean, play the ball about a ball-width back from where you normally play it and stand a little taller at address. Limit body movement by making a three-quarter, arms-only swing. Quieting the lower body reduces clubhead speed, so take two clubs more than normal.

On the downswing, think about keeping your hands a little higher as you sweep the club through impact to prevent hitting behind the ball. Better to catch it a little thin than a little heavy.

8

TURN YOUR SLICE INTO A FADE

The fade is a great shot to have, particularly if distance is not your problem. But a gentle fade can become a slice with very little notice. Then once you have it, a slice seems to feed on itself and your adjustments seem to make it even more severe. Here are some checkpoints to help you reclaim that gentle fade.

CHECK YOUR GRIP

Strong players often fall into the habit of turning their hands too far to the left on the club, possibly to prevent hooking. This weak grip makes it difficult to get the clubface back to square at impact, and the ball slides off the open clubface to the right. So place your hands on the club in a neutral position, with the back of the left hand and palm of the right facing the target. The Vs formed by the thumbs and forefingers should point to the inside of your right shoulder.

LINE UP A LITTLE LEFT

Many golfers try to curve the ball by setting up with their bodies pointing drastically left or right of the target. If you're conscious of slicing, the tendency is to aim even further left to allow for it. But fight the urge to aim too far left.

Set the leading edge of your clubface square to your target. Carefully align your feet, knees, hips and shoulders just a touch left of your target line. Have a friend stand behind you to confirm your alignment. It's too easy to think you're aligning properly when you're really not, particularly when fighting a slice.

Super-weak grip leads to open clubface.

Neutral grip promotes square return of clubface through ball.

DON'T CUT IT

Once you're aligned, you simply swing the club on a normal plane relative to your body line. Don't try picking the club up and to the outside on the backswing or manipulating the clubhead from outside-in on the downswing. If you swing along the plane your body has established, the clubhead will contact the ball while moving just slightly from outside to inside the target line. When you return the clubface squarely to the ball, the shot will start slightly left of the target and drift gently right as it descends.

Keep close tabs on your grip and alignment angles and you'll be able to reproduce the controlled fade on shot after shot—and stay consistently in play.

Swing normally
and let your
setup angles
do the work
for you.

Set clubface square
to target line and
make sure your
body points just
slightly left.

9

CUTTING CORNERS

One of the big advantages of your power is that when you hit the fairway, you have a shorter second shot than most players.

This can be especially true on doglegs, where your ability to carry the ball great lengths gives you the opportunity to cut the corner, leaving a very short second shot and a better chance at birdie. This can

Secondary target

Primary target

Intermediate target

Use the "Target" routine for correct alignment when hitting over a corner.

Hole #6   Par 4

415 yds.

175 yds.

Carry 280
240

Traps -220 yds.

mean a big psychological edge over a shorter-hitting opponent, who, instead of being 10 or 15 yards behind, is 40 yards back with a long iron, while you're choosing a wedge.

BEWARE OF THE RISKS
Cutting corners is risky, even for a long hitter. The typical dogleg is designed with some type of hazard guarding the inside corner— usually water, sand or trees. So it's essential to know exactly how far you can carry the ball off the tee; not your total carry-and-roll distance, but the ball's yardage in the air.

Once you know your carry, you can determine how much of the bend you can safely bite off. This is where knowledge of each dogleg hole comes into play: Find out the yardage it takes to safely make the

fairway. Take the time to get the facts or you might turn a good opportunity into a disaster. Then the advantage swings to your opponent.

GET THE RIGHT ALIGNMENT
Although they have the necessary power, many players have problems cutting corners because they can't aim the ball away from the fairway. The fairway is a defined, visible target, while somewhere out over the trees away from a "straight" shot would seem to spell trouble.

You can overcome this fear of hitting toward an unknown landing area by developing a new setup routine. Start by picking a primary target, which is usually the hazard you plan to hit over. Next, determine your secondary target, the spot in the fairway where the ball

should land. Even if the area is obscured by trees, make an effort to visualize it and the ball landing safely in it.

To get properly aligned, imagine a straight line running from the secondary target through the primary target and back to the tee. It may help to pick out an intermediate target on the line just in front of the tee such as a leaf or spot to help you position the club and your body.

Concentrate on making solid contact. There won't be much room for a misguided shot, so give yourself some leeway in case it fails to come off exactly as planned. Don't aim for a spot so far away that you need a career drive to reach it and don't ever let the chances of catching the hazard outweigh the chances of reaching the fairway.

Keep Your Own Yardage Book

Poor club selection probably results in more missed greens than poor swing mechanics. Keep a notebook of your average carry and the total distance with every club in your bag. Also, take the time to pace off yardages on your home course. Your effort will be rewarded the next time you're uncertain of which club to use.

Club	Carry	Total Yardage
Driver	240	260
3-Wood	220	240
4-Wood	210	230
2-iron	200	210
3-iron	190	200
4-iron	182	190
5-iron	175	180
6-iron	165	170
	155	160
	147	150
9-iron	138	140
Wedge	128	130

10

KEEP YOUR BALANCE

Every golfer needs to be in balance during his swing. But balance is of extra importance to the big hitter because of his extra-long, extra-powerful motion. If his balance is off even a little at key points along the way, the bad results will be exaggerated.

A good test of your balance is how you feel at the finish of the swing. Ideally, you should end with about 95 percent of your weight balanced on the outside of the left foot. If you're teetering off your left foot at the top of the follow-through or are forced to step forward or fall backward because your weight has moved too far onto the toes or heels, you've got a balance problem. The results of those shots probably are as shaky as your final position.

BALANCED BEGINNINGS
If you're losing your balance during the swing, you probably aren't balanced at address. Start with the feet spread shoulder-width apart: any narrower will almost guarantee you'll tip to the left or right. Distribute your weight equally between the feet. Don't put too much weight on either the balls or heels of the feet, but distribute it evenly. If you favor the balls of the feet, you'll tend to tip forward; weight on the heels pulls you back.

You should have a solid foundation. Test your balance by having someone give you a gentle push from the front, back and both sides. If you've set up properly, a light push should not move you off your feet.

You should finish your swing with 95 percent of your weight on the outside of your left foot.

STAY INSIDE
Bobby Jones once noted that golf should be played from the insides of the feet. Your weight should be centered on these two areas for most of the swing.

Guard against rolling your weight to the outside of the right foot at the top of the backswing, which almost always results in swaying. Start out at address with your right knee flexed and kicked in slightly to act as a brace against the weight shifting and keep it there throughout the backswing.

The only time your weight should move off the insides is in the follow-through and finish, when your body comes up and onto the outside of the left foot.

SWING WITHIN YOURSELF
If you lose balance after the swing and fall off your left foot, you may be swinging too hard for your own good. Tour players generally swing at about 80 percent of their total power so they can retain control. The temptation is always great to take a big cut at it, but you'll be more effective if you "stay within yourself." You'll make a more controlled swing, which means squarer contact.

Feet Together Drill

Here is a great drill to try that not only improves swing-balance, but also forces you to swing within yourself. Simply practice hitting balls with your feet together. A few minutes a day doing this will also work wonders for your swing tempo.

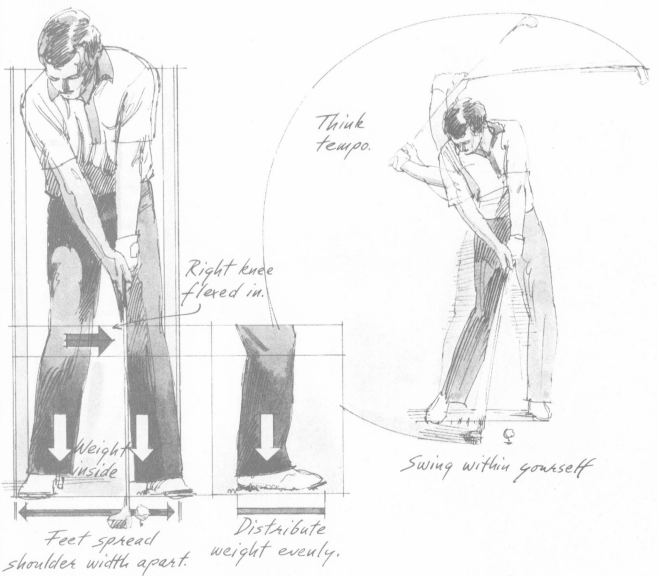

Right knee flexed in.

Think tempo.

Weight inside

Swing within yourself

Feet spread shoulder width apart.

Distribute weight evenly.

11

CRISPER CHIPS AND PITCHES

If your shots regularly sail off-line between tee and green, it's to your advantage to be able to get the ball up and down. Power hitters as a rule have few problems hitting the ball solidly (though wildly) on full-swing shots, but sometimes they have trouble making solid contact with finesse shots—chips and pitches. The combination of an errant approach with a thinned or chili-dipped short shot is bound to produce at least a bogey, if not worse. The following tips may help you make crisper contact on chips and pitches.

DOWNWARD BLOW PREVENTS FAT SHOTS

Hitting a short shot fat (so it falls well short of your target) may be caused by several faults. One is trying to help the ball into the air by scooping under it.

To get the ball airborne on a short shot you have to hit down on it with a descending blow, hitting the ball first and trusting the club's loft the same way you would with a full-force shot.

First, be sure your setup promotes striking the ball with a firm, downward blow. Your stance should be narrow (about three inches at the heels for chips; six inches for pitches), with the ball no farther forward than your left heel. Choke down on the shaft to increase clubhead control. Hands should be even with or slightly ahead of the ball—not behind it. Finally, focus your attention on the front of the ball, not the back, and let the hands lead the clubhead through impact.

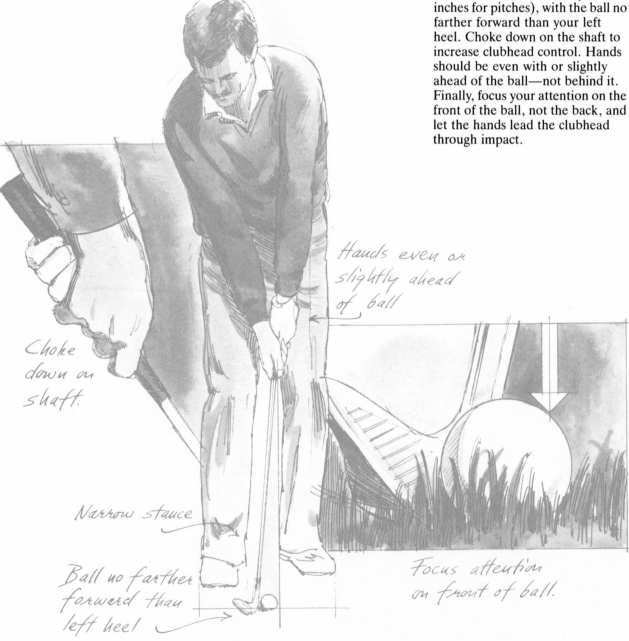

Hands even or slightly ahead of ball

Choke down on shaft.

Narrow stance

Ball no farther forward than left heel

Focus attention on front of ball.

To ensure good balance stay crouched and keep your knees flexed through impact.

Left Hand Only Drill: Although the short shots require only short swings, you still need all the clubhead control you can get. To build control and feel, choke down and practice hitting chips and pitches using your left hand only. Hit a few shots, then use both hands again. Club control will feel much sharper and positive.

CROUCH MORE TO STOP THINNED SHOTS

A "thin" chip or pitch happens when the club's leading edge hits the ball just below its equator, causing the shot to fly lower and harder than normal. A thinned short shot comes from the same source as a thin full shot: The upper body rises as the club swings forward, lifting the downswing arc so the leading edge of the club strikes high on the ball.

Rising on the shot usually is caused by standing too straight at address. Be sure to get into a good crouch, flexing your knees and bending well at the waist. Weight should be balanced between the feet as well as between the heels and balls of the feet. Imagine resting your chin on a shelf and keep it there—don't lift it—as you swing back and through. Also, be sure the ball lies between your left heel and the center of your stance and isn't too far back.

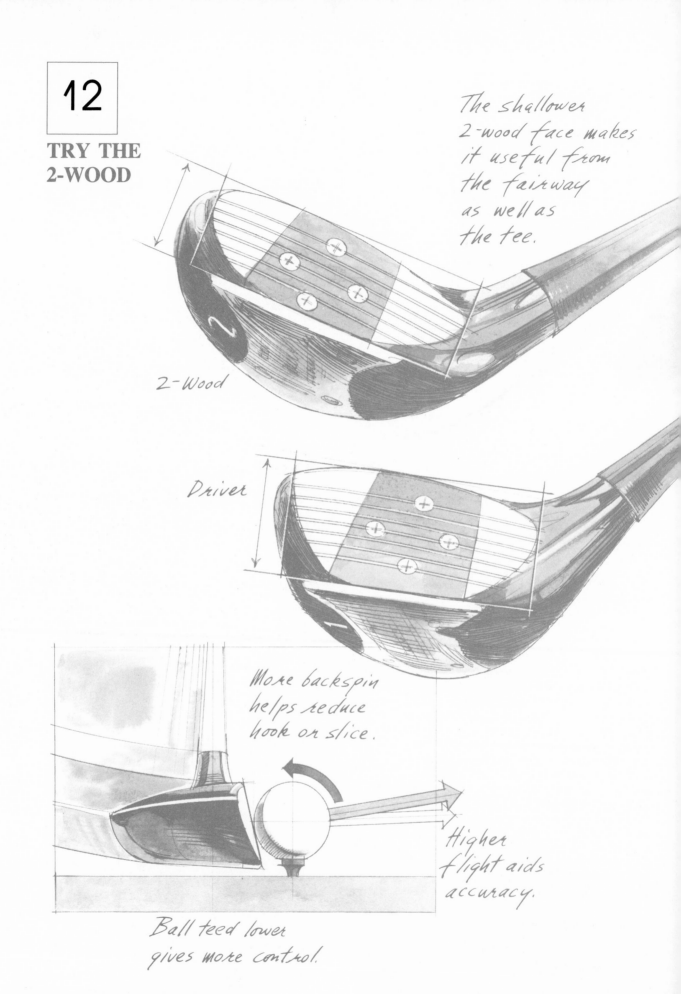

12

TRY THE 2-WOOD

The shallower 2-wood face makes it useful from the fairway as well as the tee.

2-Wood

Driver

More backspin helps reduce hook or slice.

Higher flight aids accuracy.

Ball teed lower gives more control.

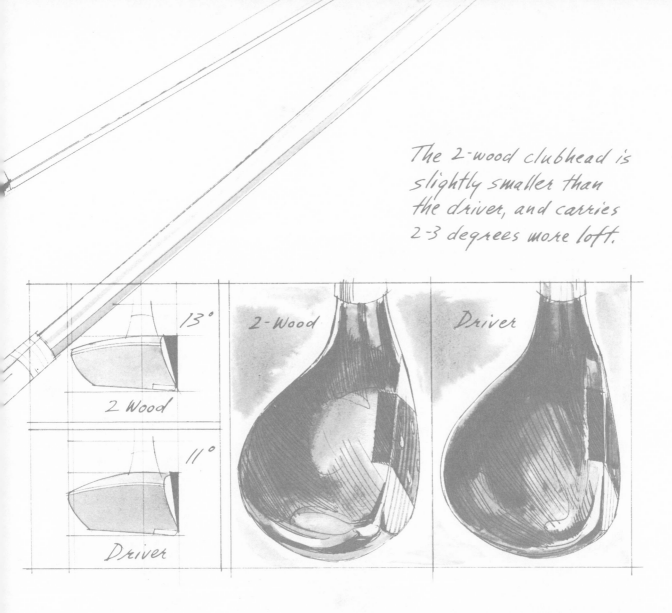

The 2-wood clubhead is slightly smaller than the driver, and carries 2-3 degrees more loft.

13° 2 Wood

11° Driver

2-Wood

Driver

No rule says you have to hit a driver off the tee on every par four and par five. If you're hitting the ball long but not straight, an alternative club off the tee might be the answer. But if teeing off with a 3-wood means you will give up too much distance, consider the "forgotten" club, the 2-wood.

EXTRA LOFT AIDS ACCURACY

The 2-wood carries about 13 degrees of loft compared to the 10 or 11 degrees of most drivers. This extra loft gives the ball a slightly higher flight, an aid to accuracy because the ball won't run as far as it would off the driver. This limitation is especially helpful when hitting to sloping fairways. The

added loft of the 2-wood also imparts more backspin on the ball. Because backspin reduces the effect of a hook or slice spin, the shot will not curve as much. You benefit two ways with added loft: Less chance of rolling into trouble and less chance of a bad hook or slice.

SHORTER SHAFT, SHALLOWER CLUBFACE

The shaft of the 2-wood, being marginally shorter than that of the driver, will cost you a few yards. But the shorter shaft makes square contact with the ball easier. If you tend to hit the ball all over the clubface, the additional control from the 2-wood will prove a genuine benefit.

Because the 2-wood also has a shallower clubface, you can tee the ball a little lower yet get plenty of height on the shot. The lower you tee the ball, the more you'll have control. Nor will you feel you have to "muscle" your tee shot with the smaller clubhead.

With no wind, you'll hit the 2-wood 12-15 yards shorter than your driver, assuming you hit both clubs equally well. When the wind's at your back, you'll hit the 2-wood *farther* than the driver because the extra loft on the face will lift the ball more quickly into the air, allowing it to ride the wind. But hitting into the wind with the 2-wood will appreciably shorten yardage; the ball's higher flight will make it more susceptible to the wind's force.

13

HOW TO JUDGE
THE ROUGH

Take time to analyze your lie.

Even short rough can be a nightmare when wet.

As a power hitter, your mishits are going to travel further off-line than your shorter hitting counterpart. While this isn't earth-shattering news, the fact remains that your power will probably put you in the rough several times during a normal round. By learning how the rough affects your shots, you can minimize the penalty imposed by your errant drives.

WET IS WORSE THAN DRY
The length of rough your ball lies in is just one consideration in analyzing your shot. A second consideration is the moisture content of the grass—how wet is it? Dry rough is much easier to play out of than wet rough. In certain cases, you can play a normal approach shot from the rough if the grass is dry and brittle, for it will have little effect on the clubface as you swing into the ball. Conversely, two-inch, wet rough can be a nightmare. The moisture thickens the grass, which slows the clubhead, so be ready to take more club in this case. Wet rough also reduces backspin, resulting in a "knuckle-ball" effect as the ball flies from this type of lie, so plan for some roll.

Ball nestled at bottom of rough... chop down sharply.

LIE AFFECTS THE SHOT

How deep the ball lies in the rough has a major affect on both the distance and backspin of your shot. If the ball is sitting up on top of the grass where you can get most of the clubface on the back of it, then you can play a basically normal approach. But the deeper the ball lies, the more clubhead speed and backspin will be reduced. When the ball is nestled way down, plan to chop down on it with a more lofted club, playing for a minimum of carry and a maximum of roll.

Above all, realize your limitations and take the club that will ensure getting you out safely. You're better off hitting a 7-iron to the front of the green than leaving a 4-iron in the high grass.

14

TENSION TAMERS: THE WAGGLE AND FORWARD PRESS

How you start the swing determines the rhythm and tempo that follow. If you start by jerking the club back, the rest of the swing will be uneven. A smooth take-away, however, ensures a smooth swing. The power hitter who sprays the ball can build control by smoothing out the rough, bumpy parts of his swing, particularly the takeaway. An easy way to make an even, relaxed start is by employing a waggle and forward press.

THE WAGGLE
The waggle is a simple working of the clubhead back and forth with the hands and wrists before the takeaway. The waggle relaxes the small muscles in the hands, allowing you to feel the clubhead and stay in motion while preparing for the shot. The waggle should be smooth and rhythmic, just the way you want your takeaway to be. Furthermore, the clubhead should waggle on the same line as the takeaway, moving slightly inside going back. If you're loose, you'll feel the clubhead from your fingers up to the shoulders.

Use small muscles of wrists and hands.

Waggle should be smooth and rhythmic.

Club moves to inside.

THE FORWARD PRESS

After loosening up with a waggle, place the clubhead behind the ball and bring the body into a set position for a second before starting the swing. Because freezing the body, even momentarily, invites tension, it's wise to incorporate a forward press—a slight movement of some part of the body—to break tension and trigger the swing. The pros employ a variety of presses: Jack Nicklaus turns his head slightly away from the ball, Gary Player slides his right knee toward the target, Greg Norman pushes the club slightly away from his body (squaring the face behind the ball). You want to find some little move that is both comfortable and breaks the tension. Just be sure your trigger doesn't set you up for a fault: For example, some players push their hands forward; going too far forward might set up an early wrist cock that will inhibit a full swing.

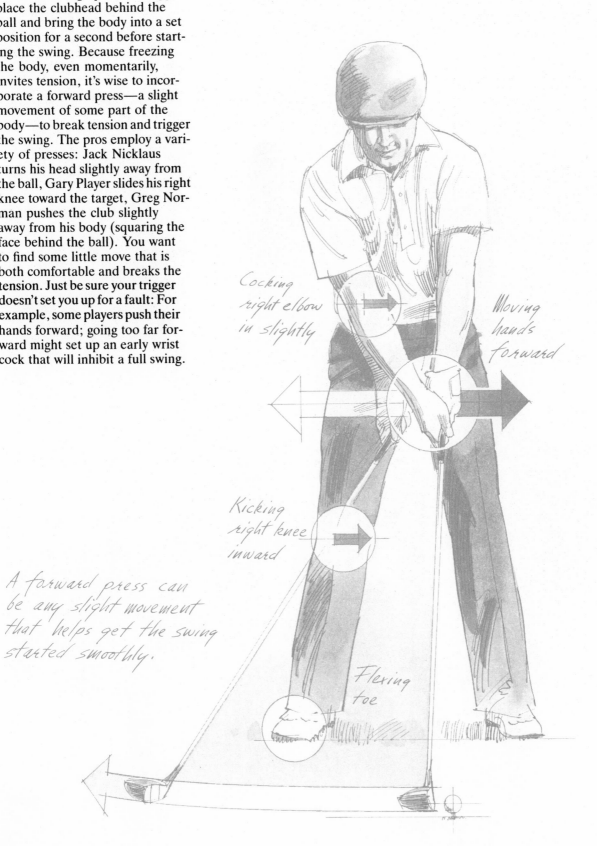

Cocking right elbow in slightly

Moving hands forward

Kicking right knee inward

A forward press can be any slight movement that helps get the swing started smoothly.

Flexing toe

15

WHEN THE WHEELS FALL OFF

Every golfer has rounds that get off to a promising start then unravel until nothing goes right. By the final tee, nearly every shot—even those normally handled with ease—seems hard. Pros speak of "the wheels falling off," and it happens to everyone.

When your game falls apart, you either can give up and leave the course angry or you can make the best of the round and perhaps learn a thing or two that will help you the next time.

Some days it seems you can't do anything right!

Make sure you aren't exaggerating one of your swing keys.

PRELUDE TO A FALL

Since you probably are a little wild off the tee to begin with, your shots fly even farther astray when the wheels fall off. To keep that from happening, you have to find out what you're doing wrong.

Start by checking that you aren't exaggerating a swing key. Say your downswing key is to drive your hips toward the target. Early in the round you hit the ball well holding that thought. Then you started thinking that a stronger lower-body drive would hit the ball farther. But too much lower-body motion can cause upper-body movement, which leads to poor impact. Suddenly you're driving your hips and hitting pulls and slices. Be careful not to exaggerate any part of your swing.

CHOKE DOWN OR BACK DOWN

Suppose you're unable to pinpoint a specific fault during the round. You still can contain the damage by getting some control on your shots. Choke down on every club except the putter. Not a lot: Half an inch should do. But that half inch could save you 10 yards right or left. If choking down doesn't help, try backing down: Hit a 3-wood or less off the tee; don't hit woods and long irons from the fairway when hitting to a high-risk target.

SHORT GAME SAVES

Don't lose heart. Skilled players know nothing is more challenging than trying to save a score when the game isn't there. Instead of resigning yourself to a poor score, try salvaging holes with your short game. Grind on chips, pitches and putts rather than giving up. Once a break or two goes your way, you may suddenly find that missing swing and be back on track.

Work hard on pitches and chips.

Back down on club selection.

Try choking down on club.

16

LOUSY LIES

The ball's position in mud determines the shot.

Off-line hits mean you're going to face some "lousy" lies, situations far more troublesome than a typical rough shot or sand blast. Here's how to handle a few shots from off the beaten track.

Firm grip

Open stance

MUD
A ball sitting cleanly on mud should be played like a fairway bunker shot. Sweep the ball cleanly off the surface: Stand a little taller by reducing your knee flex and place the ball a half inch behind your normal position to ensure hitting the ball first. For middle irons, long irons and fairway woods, make a very low takeaway; for short irons make your normal swing. An additional tip: Hover the head behind the ball at address to avoid snagging the club in the muck on the takeaway.

A plugged ball has to be exploded loose. Play it like a buried lie in a trap: Open your stance, close the clubface and take a firm grip. Club selection depends on the depth the ball is buried. If it's only slightly below the surface, a mid or even long iron may work. A deeper lie requires a short iron, probably a pitching wedge. Never use a sand wedge; its big flange will mire in the heavy muck.

Plugged ball

ROOTS

A ball resting against a tree root may be better left unplayed. Smacking a club into a hard and immovable root could result in injury to your hands or wrists and/or a broken club.

If you do decide to play the shot, the ball's position becomes the key. Since it's hard to get the clubface on a ball sitting just in front of a root, consider hitting an intentional "top" with your putter: Its short shaft aids control and its straight face will impart topspin for a lot of roll.

A root in front of your ball is a potential danger. Trapping the ball between tree and club will cause the ball to fly straight up or back into you (and if it touches you, it's a two-shot penalty). If you decide to play it, take a wedge and punch the ball out with an easy swing; anything harder invites injury. Another option is to hit the shot laterally.

A root to the side of the ball outside the target line poses the least amount of trouble since you can make contact, albeit off the toe. Stand a half inch farther from the ball than usual and hold the club a little tighter to keep it from twisting in your hands at impact.

A root inside the target line forces you to address the ball off the hosel, begging for a shank. Again, your best bet is to take the putter and try running the ball back to safety. You might also try turning a wedge over and swinging left-handed. Or, an option in all these cases, face the music and take an unplayable lie.

Top ball with putter

Root behind the ball

Easy punch with wedge

Root in front of the ball

Hit ball with toe of club

Root outside the ball

Play wedge left-handed

Root inside the ball

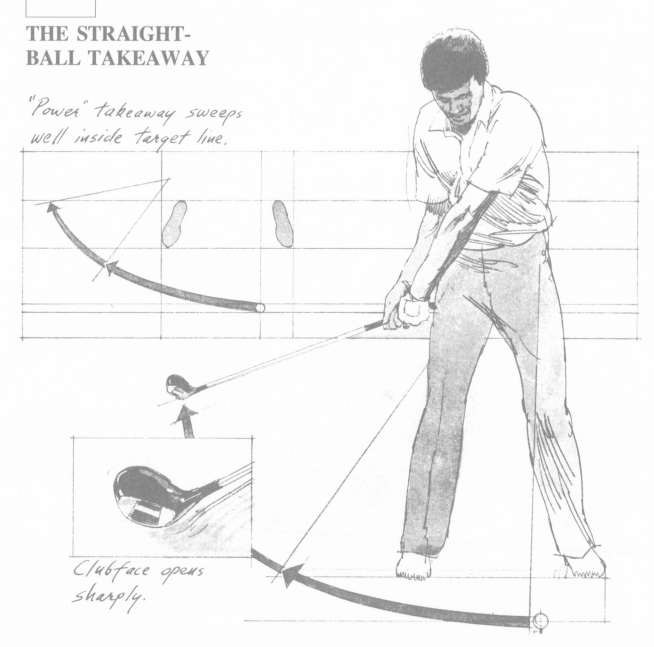

17

THE STRAIGHT-BALL TAKEAWAY

"Power" takeaway sweeps well inside target line.

Clubface opens sharply.

If you're hitting your drives a long way but spraying them from side to side, the cure may lie in your takeaway—specifically within the first foot-and-a-half from the ball.

For many golfers, how the club approaches the ball at impact mirrors the takeaway. Power hitters tend to pull the driver sharply inside the target line in the takeaway. Consequently, the clubhead approaches impact from the inside, moves down the line and

returns to inside on the follow-through. This inside-to-inside path promotes power for two reasons. First, the clubhead comes to the ball on a level path; second, the inside takeaway fans the clubface open in the takeaway. On the return the face moves quickly from open to square to closed, putting right-to-left spin on the ball for more distance.

At least that's the theory. You'll get the booming tee shot only when

your timing is perfect and the club travels down the line at impact with a square clubface. But perfection is elusive: If either the clubhead path or clubface is off by even a hair, the result will be a mix of erratic shots, mostly hooks and pushes. One of the best ways to keep the clubhead closer to the target line and reduce the chance of a misaligned clubface is by adopting the straight-back takeaway.

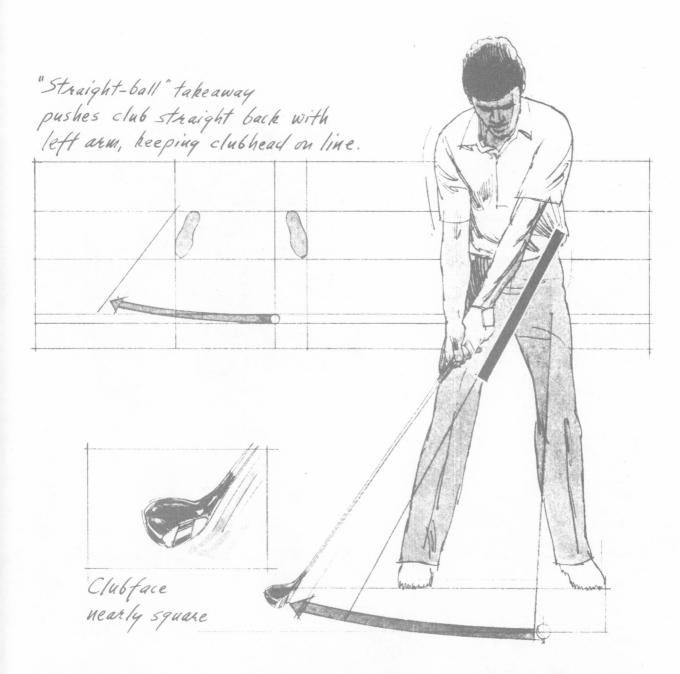

"Straight-ball" takeaway pushes club straight back with left arm, keeping clubhead on line.

Clubface nearly square

PULL CLUB BACK WITH LEFT SIDE

The first 18 inches of the takeaway is the key. Envision a foot-and-a-half line straight back from the ball and pull the clubhead slowly over that line with your hands. Your left hand, arm and shoulder move as a unit in setting the club in motion. Move the club back as slowly as you can to promote balance in the lower body and also to encourage a strong turning of the upper body in the backswing.

Starting the club straight along the target line should mean the club will return straight along the line for that crucial one foot on either side of the ball. Also, because the clubface won't fan open quite as much on the takeaway, you won't have to force a release of the hands to square up at impact.

This "straight-ball" takeaway alters the plane of your driver, making it more upright. The clubhead will come into the ball on a steeper angle, so ball position must be just right if you're going to hit the ball "dead level." You may lose a few yards if you catch the ball a shade on the downswing or upswing, but the increased accuracy more than outweighs any small distance loss. Remember, too, that a drive in the fairway rolls much farther than one in the rough.

18

SPANK THE SHORT SAND SHOT

Right hand controls downswing.

"Spank" the sand just behind the ball.

There's a tendency among power hitters to think in terms of "exploding" the ball out of the bunker, taking loads of sand no matter what the length of the shot or the lie. There's no need for this when the lie is good and you only have, say, 15 feet to the green and another 15 feet to the hole.

You have to put spin on this shot so the ball pops up quickly and lands softly. This is accomplished by taking *less* sand, not more.

Start by addressing the ball with both stance and the face of the sand wedge open. The shorter the shot the more open both your stance and your blade should be. Play the ball opposite your left heel, with the leading edge of the wedge an inch behind the ball. Your weight should slightly favor your left foot. Swing back along your body line (outside-in relative to the target line) in an upright arc. You should feel that your right hand is controlling the movement and cocking the club up.

As you swing down, try to "spank" the sand behind the ball sharply with your right hand. The open clubface will facilitate "skimming" rather than digging; the back of the flange enters the sand first, so the leading edge can't dig.

Keep in mind that the *rear* of the flange hits the sand first and that the leading edge is approximately three-fourths of an inch closer to the ball. So spank the sand far enough behind the ball to avoid hitting it with the leading edge, resulting in a skull.

Your hands should come up to an abrupt follow-through after spanking the sand. The ball will pop up and carry plenty of spin because the sand is lifting and rotating the ball from *underneath* rather than well behind it.

Practice to find the right amount of backswing to cover the distance to the flag while planning to hit a consistent distance behind the ball. Once you ingrain the feel for the swing and the distance, you should expect to put this shot within one-putt range every time.

Back of flange makes contact; sand
under ball rotates ball backward for
strong spinning action.

19

THE LOW SHOT
UNDER TREES

If you're not in the fairway, at least some of each round is spent in and under trees. Here's how to hit the "under-the-tree" shot to help you get back into play.

CHECK OUT THE BRANCHES
Assume the tree or trees blocking your way are too high to shoot over. You may have to punch the shot underneath them. But before you do, study the branches. If you can't advance the ball very far going the low route but the branches are thin and spread out, you might hit through them. Try this shot only when there are no nearby out-of-bounds, water hazards or thick woods.

TAKE A SIDE VIEW
If going under the branches is the

Study the trajectory you need from the side.

Grip down

Play a longer iron back in your stance, hands ahead with weight left.

choice, be sure to scout the situation from the side. This view shows how low the ball must fly, which helps determine the right club. If the branches are 30 feet in front of you and six feet off the ground, a 4-iron may be the most lofted club you can take.

KNOW THE LIE

To estimate the starting trajectory of the shot, you have to know how the ball will come off its lie. You're better off if it's on hardpan or very thin grass because you can hood the blade and easily hit a lower-than-normal shot. Getting out of heavy rough, though, will require a more lofted club to dig the ball out, so it's tougher to keep the shot low.

Also, check the grass *beyond* the tree. Can you get back on the fairway or will heavy rough stop you dead?

HIT DOWN HARD

Set up with your weight on your left side, the ball back of center in your stance and your hands well ahead. This encourages hooding the blade for a low shot. Grip down on the club for control and a narrow arc, which also help keep the ball down.

Swing back to a three-quarter position with your arms but don't break the wrists. At the top, your weight should be more on your left side than usual.

Pull the club down and through, leading with your hands through impact. This ensures a descending clubhead at impact and helps start the ball low. Finish low in the punch position, arms and clubshaft pointing at the target.

Finish low in "punch" position, with arms and clubshaft pointing at target.

Three-quarter swing position with no wrist break.

20

PUT SOME PUNCH IN YOUR GAME

The mid-iron punch is a control shot that goes the same distance but flies lower than a typical short-iron.

Three-quarter arm swing

Club delofted.

Play the ball just behind center.

Most amateur power players don't think enough about control. From driver to sand wedge, they employ the same big swing with only one thought in mind: Boom it! But accuracy, and therefore the score, is sacrificed. If this sounds like you, trade a little length for control by learning the middle-iron "punch."

PLAYING THE PUNCH

The object of the punch shot is to send the ball a precise distance on a straight line, but with an easier swing than your normal brutish blast. The shot will fly lower and shorter and, unlike other low shots, won't run too far after landing. As an example, if you have 150 yards to a green flanked by bunkers on both sides, trade your regular 8-iron, which might fade or draw into trouble, for an easy, punched 6-iron that flies true.

Play the ball back just behind center. This takes a little loft off the club, which makes the ball fly lower, and promotes "ball-first" contact for more backspin. Swing mainly with your arms, no farther than three-quarters, and keep your wrists firm and hands quiet on the downswing and through impact. The follow-through will be low and short, limited by the force of the swing.

The successful punch depends on smooth rhythm, crucial so you don't decelerate into the ball. Make a few practice swings, striving for a pendulum motion back and through. Try to duplicate that easy rhythm on the real thing. Don't hurry or jump at the ball.

MIND GAMES

For most power hitters, who swing hard at almost everything, making a smooth, rhythmic swing means changing the way they think. Suddenly, golf is not merely a power game.

The punch is a control shot, when you want to hit the ball an exact distance, not maximum distance. Practicing the punch conditions your mind to accept a different way of playing, one that will improve your accuracy and score.

Keep the wrists firm and the hands quiet on the downswing.

Follow-through is low and short, limited by the force of the swing.

21

"FRINGE" PUTTS

Your stroke mechanics don't change for a putt from the fringe. Assume your normal grip and address position. Sole the putter very lightly or not at all; this ensures that your takeaway will be smooth, even if the ground behind the ball isn't.

Concentrate on making a level stroke, with the putter hitting the center of the ball. This will keep "bouncing" to a minimum. ■

Think about the number of times you get up and down from off the edge of the green. If you don't hole out in two nearly every time, you're throwing away strokes.

Do you automatically reach for a lofted club from a short distance off the green? Here are several reasons for putting from off the green whenever you have the chance:

1. *It's easier to judge the speed of a rolling ball.* To prove it, drop a few balls near the edge of a green. Putt them to a hole 30-40 feet away, then pitch with a sand wedge so that the balls fly most of the way. Which shots, on average, were closer to the right length?

2. *A putt is more accurate than a chip.* You'll keep the ball on line better, so the possibility of holing the shot increases. Also, it's easier to stroke a solid putt than a solid chip.

3. *Most players are more aggressive with the putter.* If you chip, you'll probably be thinking of just getting close. Putt the identical shot and you're likely to focus more intently on knocking the ball into the hole. You should approach both shots in the same way, but you're more conditioned to think "sink" with the putter.

When to putt it? If the ball is lying cleanly within two feet of the green and the distance to the putting surface is free of bumps, long grass or very soft turf.

You can putt from farther off the green as well. If the ground is flat and firm and the grass dry and short, use the putter even from 10 or more yards off—the "Texas Wedge." This tactic is especially helpful in windy conditions, particularly downhill and downwind when it's harder to stop the ball.

Dry conditions call for the putter from short distances off the green.

Straight Hitter

You keep the ball in play most of the time, but a lack of distance puts pressure on your game.

Golf is a game of distance and direction, which means the straight hitter has half the battle won. It's rare to see this guy (or gal—many women fall into this category) stray too far off the fairway. But he's almost always the farthest from the green and hard-pressed to reach it in two on any but the shortest par fours. That puts him at a big disadvantage on many courses, especially long, "championship" layouts and those demanding long carries over sand or water.

The straight hitter usually makes a consistent, rhythmic swing, but one lacking in strength. Not surprisingly, then, the major purpose of the instruction that follows is acquiring extra distance, finding ways to add power without sacrificing control. A number of distance-robbing faults are analyzed, as are specific shots and equipment choices that will boost yardage.

A lack of length also means the straight hitter must have terrific touch—in the short game and on the greens—if he hopes to shoot low scores. Pars and birdies usually come as a result of deft play with the wedges and the putter. With a little bit of work, the straight hitter can go a long way.

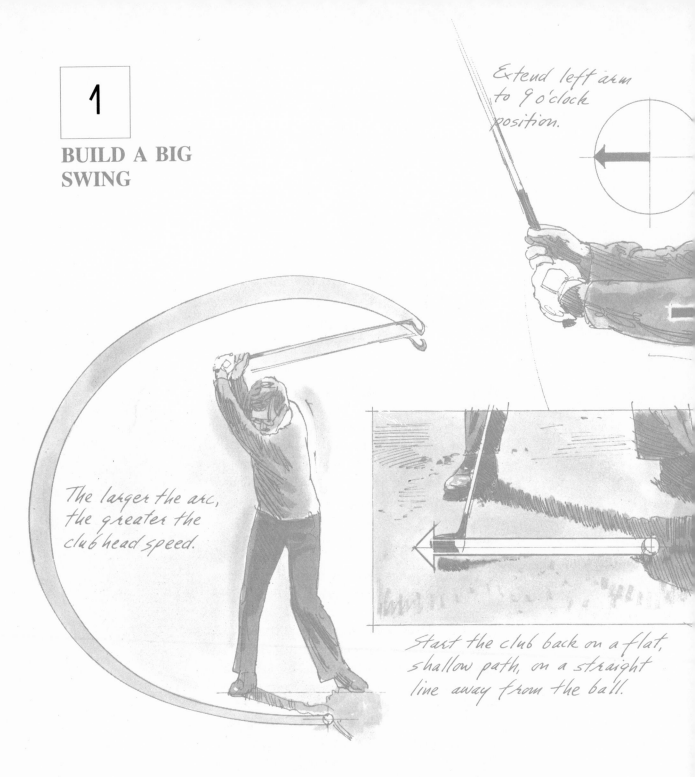

1

BUILD A BIG SWING

Extend left arm to 9 o'clock position.

The larger the arc, the greater the club head speed.

Start the club back on a flat, shallow path, on a straight line away from the ball.

A compact, controlled swing lets you keep the ball in play, but it doesn't go miles down the fairway. You can build a bigger swing— one that generates more clubhead speed—if you're willing to trade a little control for more yardage.

WIDEN YOUR ARC
Don't confuse building a bigger swing with making a longer backswing. The object is to widen the

arc on which the clubhead travels so the clubhead moves in a bigger circle.

A wide arc begins with the takeaway. Set up with a firm, not stiff, left side and slowly push the clubhead away from the ball on a straight line. (It helps if you think of the clubhead as a heavy chunk of lead.) Keep the clubhead moving on a straight line as long as you can (about a foot-and-a-half is

good) by keeping your left arm extended and letting your right arm fold under.

As your shoulders turn, the club naturally moves to the inside. Extend your left arm straight back until it's halfway back—at the 9 o'clock position. Guard against reaching too much, which results in swaying off the ball, by keeping your weight on the inside of your right foot.

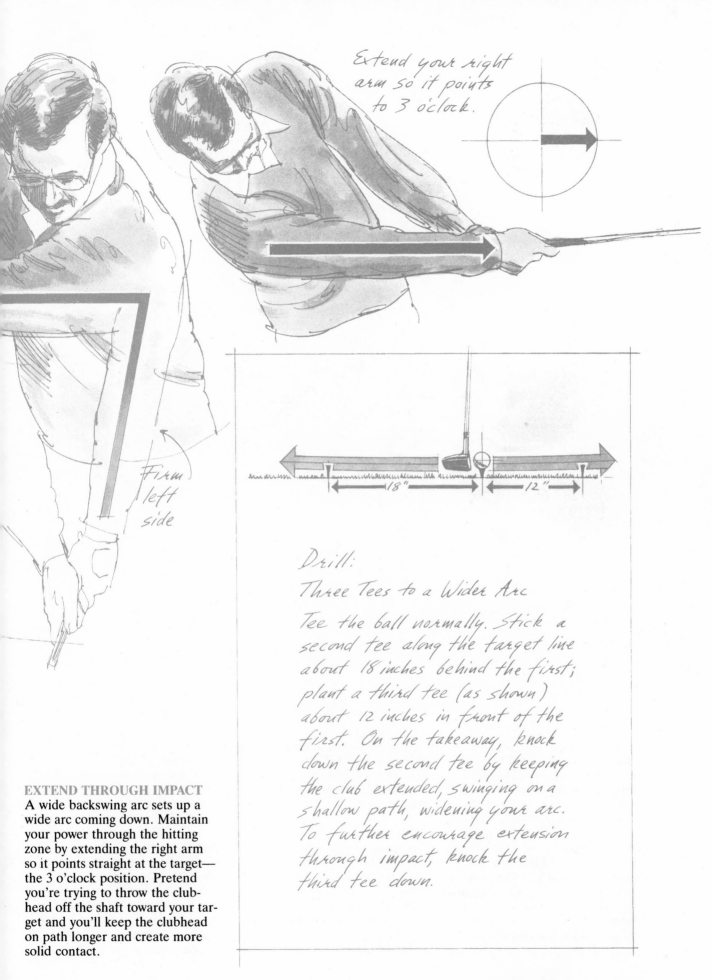

Extend your right arm so it points to 3 o'clock.

Firm left side

EXTEND THROUGH IMPACT

A wide backswing arc sets up a wide arc coming down. Maintain your power through the hitting zone by extending the right arm so it points straight at the target—the 3 o'clock position. Pretend you're trying to throw the club-head off the shaft toward your target and you'll keep the clubhead on path longer and create more solid contact.

18"

12"

Drill:

Three Tees to a Wider Arc

Tee the ball normally. Stick a second tee along the target line about 18 inches behind the first; plant a third tee (as shown) about 12 inches in front of the first. On the takeaway, knock down the second tee by keeping the club extended, swinging on a shallow path, widening your arc. To further encourage extension through impact, knock the third tee down.

2

CORRECT HEAD
POSITIONING

At address, keep your chin up and point it behind the ball.

The key ingredient to distance is clubhead speed, and one way to get more power in your swing is a bigger shoulder turn. But how far you can turn your shoulders depends on many things—age, flexibility and technique among them. It may be that you're capable of making a fuller shoulder turn than you think. The secret is using your head, more specifically the way you position your head at address. Two common flaws in head position will inhibit your shoulder turn: 1) burying your chin in your chest, and 2) pointing your chin at or left of the ball. Let's see how each mistake restricts the shoulders and how to correct them.

KEEP YOUR CHIN UP
Dropping your chin against your chest limits how far you can turn your shoulders going back. See for yourself: Try making a backswing with your chin tucked in. You can turn the shoulders only about 45 degrees before your chin hits your left shoulder, which means you're

stopping the backswing coil far short of your real limit.

If you try pushing your backswing past where the chin hits your shoulder, you force the head to the right. Moving the head effectively stops the turning and starts you swaying to the right, which makes it almost impossible to return the clubhead squarely at impact.

TILT CHIN TO THE RIGHT
Many top players, including Tour pros, start their backswing by cocking their heads right. Or they

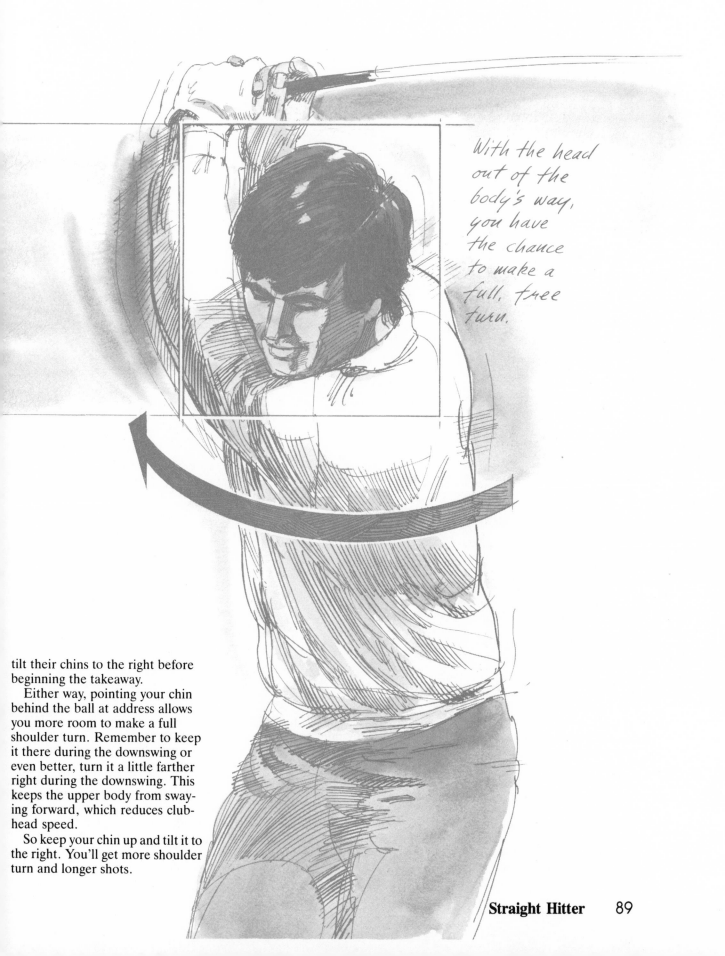

With the head out of the body's way, you have the chance to make a full, free turn.

tilt their chins to the right before beginning the takeaway.

Either way, pointing your chin behind the ball at address allows you more room to make a full shoulder turn. Remember to keep it there during the downswing or even better, turn it a little farther right during the downswing. This keeps the upper body from swaying forward, which reduces club-head speed.

So keep your chin up and tilt it to the right. You'll get more shoulder turn and longer shots.

3

HOW TO BEAT A BOMBER

Don't be trapped into trying to keep up with his distance.

If you like to compete, you're sure to find yourself pitted against a player who hits the ball much longer than you do. Although you may seem to be the underdog in this "David and Goliath" match-up, the advantage actually can be yours if you adopt the right attitude and strategy.

Tell yourself the pressure is on *him*, not you. The long-ball hitter is expected to have the edge because of the difference in distance. He probably senses this, so he may be nervous about the possibility of losing to a shorter hitter.

PLAY YOUR GAME
No matter what happens, stick to your game. Don't fall into the trap of trying to keep up with your opponent; this is what he wants.

Don't try to out-muscle a muscle man. Concentrate on keeping your tempo smooth and hitting the ball your usual length.

Play your normal, down-the-middle game, and he may end up losing his composure, especially if he's wild. But trying to keep up with his length will definitely put the strain on your game and swing the advantage to him.

Play your normal down-the-middle game.

Your short game is your equalizer— practice, practice, practice.

You'll be first to hit the approach shot on most holes, but this can be an advantage if you put the ball close. Then the target looks a lot smaller to him, putting more pressure on his shot. Even if you're not close to the pin but just on the green, he's still being squeezed.

Consequently, however, if you badly miss the green, his confidence will rise. So do all you can to keep the heat on him by putting your approaches close.

WIN AROUND THE GREENS
Since he'll probably be hitting shorter clubs than you on approach shots, your rival should have an easier time hitting greens—unless he puts himself in jail off the tee. So your short game has to be the equalizer, if not the giant-slayer.

Pitching, chipping and putting have to be your strength. If you can save a lot of pars by getting up and down, you'll drive your opponent crazy and increase your chances of winning the match.

So practice, practice and practice some more. Remember: It isn't how but how many.

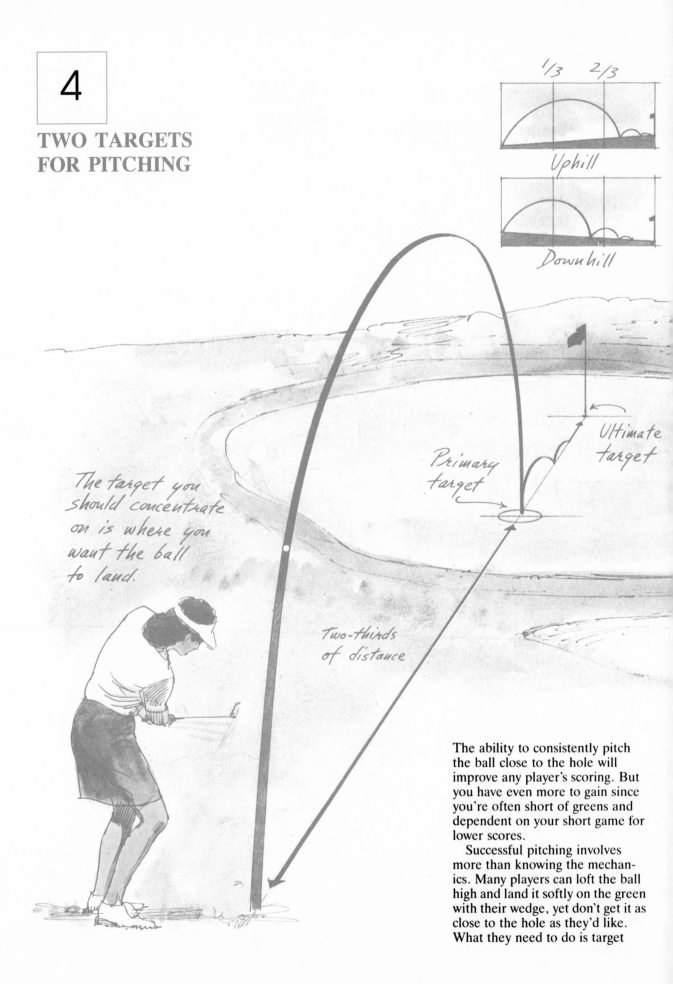

4

TWO TARGETS
FOR PITCHING

1/3 2/3

Uphill

Downhill

*Ultimate
target*

*Primary
target*

*The target you
should concentrate
on is where you
want the ball
to land.*

*Two-thirds
of distance*

The ability to consistently pitch
the ball close to the hole will
improve any player's scoring. But
you have even more to gain since
you're often short of greens and
dependent on your short game for
lower scores.

Successful pitching involves
more than knowing the mechanics. Many players can loft the ball
high and land it softly on the green
with their wedge, yet don't get it as
close to the hole as they'd like.
What they need to do is target

Two-Target Scorecard Drill

To help yourself zero in on a specific landing area for short pitches, try the following drill. Pick a spot just off the practice green to pitch from. Determine a spot about 2/3's of the distance between the ball and the cup. Mark the spot by laying a scorecard there and pushing a tee through it into the green to hold it in place. Practice hitting to this specific target. Move to different places to pitch from, each time determining your target area and moving the card. During a round, imagine your target on the greens and aim for it.

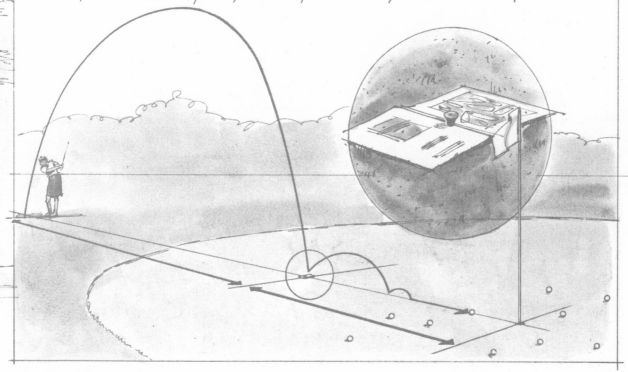

their pitches: Instead of concentrating only on where they want the ball to finish—near the hole—they must learn to consider where on the green they should make it land.

Imagine driving to a fairway that slopes severely right to left. If you want the shot to finish in the fairway, your main concern is where the ball lands so it rolls down the slope and into the center. You should plan pitch shots the same way, making the spot the ball lands on your primary concern. If you can determine correctly the best place to land the ball and know how to hit it to that spot, you'll get close more often.

PICK YOUR TARGET AREA
Most short shots played with a pitching or sand wedge will travel roughly two-thirds of the way in the air, the other third on the ground. Your primary target should be about two-thirds of the way to the hole; land the ball there, and it should roll the rest of the way.

Don't forget to consider slope. On an upslope, the ball won't roll as far, so you'll have to cover more of the distance in the air. Conversely, hitting onto a downslope creates more roll, so you need less air time. Survey the ground between ball and hole and determine whether you need more or less carry or whether the slope of the green requires you to land the ball to the right or left of the cup.

5

RELAX THE RIGHT ELBOW FOR A BIGGER TURN

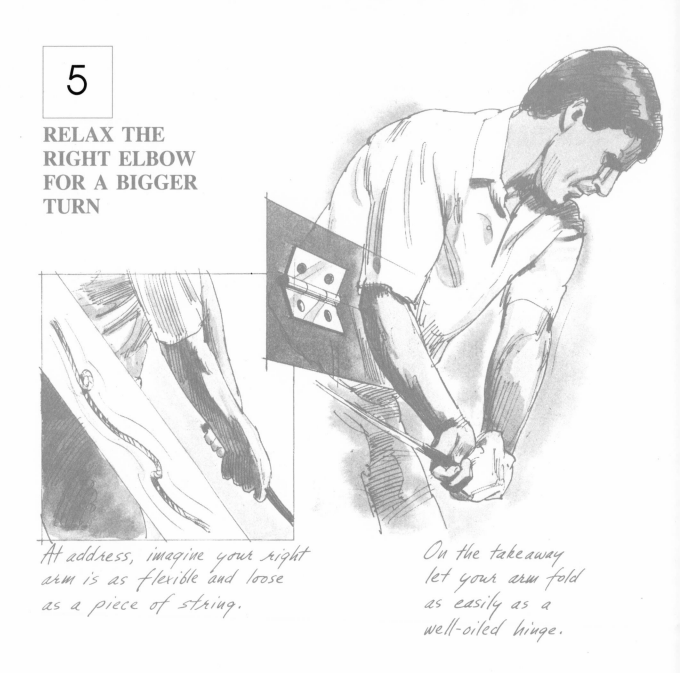

At address, imagine your right arm is as flexible and loose as a piece of string.

On the takeaway let your arm fold as easily as a well-oiled hinge.

Tension in the arms is one of the worst killers of a good swing. Even the slightest stiffness in the right elbow as you make the backswing inhibits a full shoulder turn. Consequently, the club won't fall into the proper position at the top, so you can't deliver it solidly and squarely into the ball. A restricted turn also costs distance.

LET YOUR RIGHT ELBOW FOLD

At address, your right arm should feel loose and flexible, which means letting it bend slightly at the elbow. As you move the club on the takeaway, the elbow will try to fold, and you should let it. Play-ers who fight this folding action usually do so because they sense a loss of control. Don't worry: Whether you keep the elbow close to your side or let it "fly," learn to trust that bend or you'll never make a full upper-body turn.

FEEL YOUR THUMBS

Once your right elbow starts fold-ing properly, your backswing will lengthen. At first, it may feel

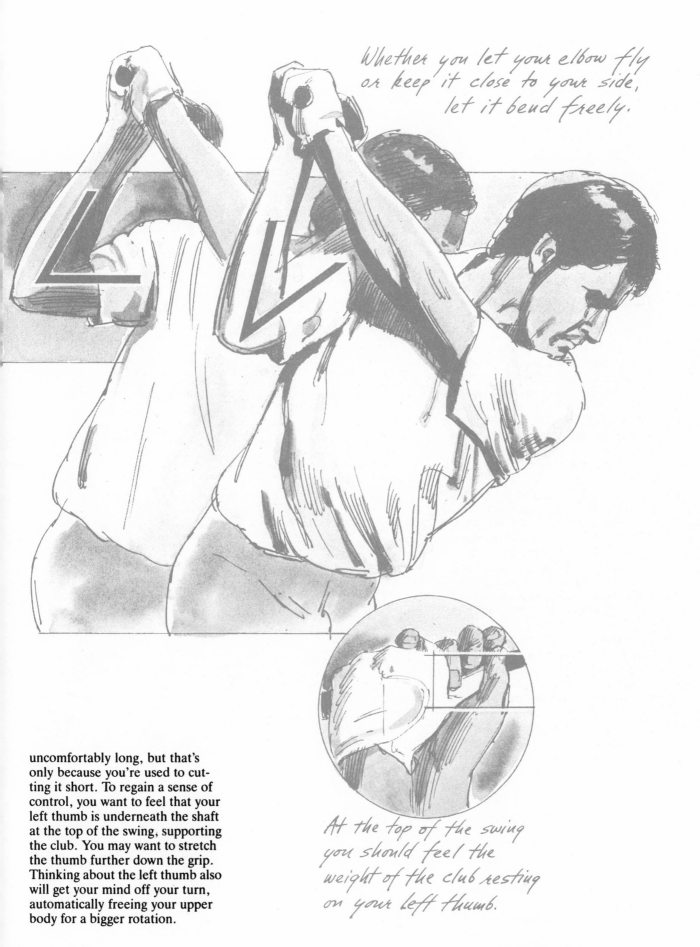

Whether you let your elbow fly or keep it close to your side, let it bend freely.

At the top of the swing you should feel the weight of the club resting on your left thumb.

uncomfortably long, but that's only because you're used to cutting it short. To regain a sense of control, you want to feel that your left thumb is underneath the shaft at the top of the swing, supporting the club. You may want to stretch the thumb further down the grip. Thinking about the left thumb also will get your mind off your turn, automatically freeing your upper body for a bigger rotation.

6

ACTIVATE YOUR FOOTWORK

You may think that to get more distance you need to lengthen the shoulder turn, cock your wrists more to create a "late hit" or somehow swing your arms faster. But don't overlook a solution to your problem that's literally at your feet—that is, improved footwork!

Few players can achieve power when relying solely on their hands and arms. Proper footwork is the key to getting leverage into your swing. It increases upper-body coil and gets more lower-body weight onto your right side, putting you in position to lead the downswing with a strong weight shift to the left.

You need to understand good footwork and practice it repeatedly, so it becomes part of your swing rather than something you need to perform consciously.

You can practice footwork anywhere, with or without a club. In fact, you'll probably learn faster if you don't practice with a golf club.

MORE BODY TURN

Start by putting your hands in front of you, palms facing as if to grip a club. Take your normal stance and place a ball opposite your left heel as a point of reference.

Your legs and feet should initiate the backswing action. Turn your left knee in toward your right knee as far as you can while keeping your right leg in place. The left knee should move eight to 10 inches to the right, so that it moves slightly behind the ball.

If you have made a full turn, your left heel will be off the ground and your weight planted firmly on your right side. Most importantly, your hips will have turned clockwise about 45

Left heel off ground

Turn left knee so that as you look down, it has moved back of the ball.

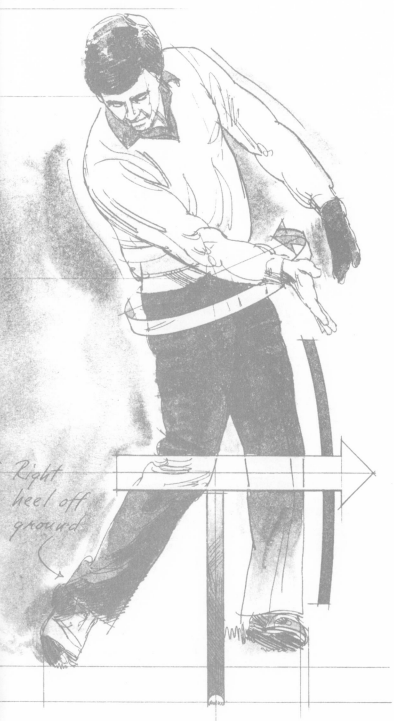

Right heel off ground

Downswing footwork includes lateral knee slide, weight on outside of left foot.

degrees. Why is this coil and hip turn so important? The more you coil your lower body, the farther you can turn your shoulders, which increases the clubhead's arc, thus its speed at impact.

If you don't believe that footwork makes a difference, try this experiment. Stand flat-footed in front of a mirror and turn only your shoulders as far as you can. It won't be very far. Now, starting with the footwork described, take your regular shoulder turn. Look how much more your upper body has coiled! Your flexibility will determine how far your shoulders turn, but good footwork will increase every golfer's coil dramatically.

SHIFT LOWER BODY FIRST

Practice making your first move down: a strong lateral shift of your knees directly toward your target. Your left knee should be bowed so that it's slightly ahead of its original address position. Your weight should be predominantly on the outside of your left foot. Your right knee will drive laterally to the left so that if you look down, it's on line with the ball. As you follow through, only a small amount of weight is on your right toe, while the right heel has been pulled off the ground.

This footwork puts leverage into your swing. The lateral shift of the knees—with the weight moving to the left side—forces the hips to unwind. Then it's a chain reaction with the torso, shoulders, arms and hands entering the downswing in that order. As a result of this pent-up energy, your wrists will snap the clubhead through impact. You'll have more clubhead speed—when it's needed.

Practice the footwork explained here and demonstrated in the drawings until it becomes second nature. Then bring it with you to the course and see your shots fly farther.

7

GETTING A
GOOD ROLL

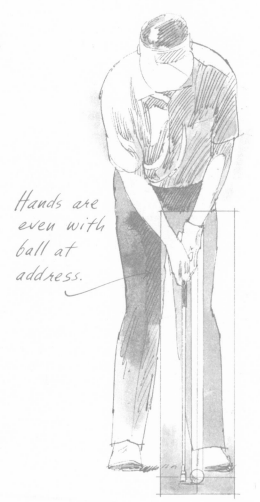

Hands are even with ball at address.

Because lack of distance puts pressure on your short game, you can't be a mediocre putter and expect to score well. Success on the greens depends on feeling the difference between merely stroking the ball and putting a good roll on it.

A GOOD ROLL STARTS AT ADDRESS

Although the putter is nicknamed the "flatstick" because its face doesn't appear to have any loft, it actually does have three or four degrees. This slight upward angle is essential to getting the ball rolling smoothly: At impact, the ball actually is lifted slightly.

To make proper use of the loft, the hands should be even with the ball at address. If your hands move ahead of the putterhead, you'll deloft the blade. At impact, the ball will be pinched down into the turf, which can cause it to skip off line at the start.

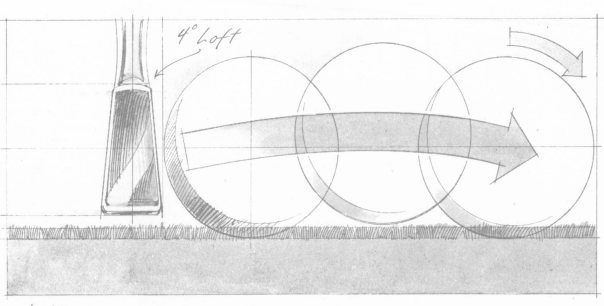

4° Loft

Loft is essential to get the ball rolling.

HIT THE SWEET SPOT

Good roll also depends on contacting the ball with the sweet spot of the putter. Hitting the ball out toward the toe imparts "hookspin" at the outset, causing the putt to move a little left. (Many amateurs make this error, which explains why most prefer putts that break from right-to-left.) Hitting the ball more toward the heel causes the opposite reaction: It puts a little "slice-spin" on the start of the roll so the putt moves right. Missing the sweet spot not only affects direction but distance: The ball won't roll as far as you expect if you don't make solid contact.

Putters generally are marked on top to indicate the location of the sweet spot. When you putt, turn the label on the ball so it points straight down the intended line, then concentrate on meeting the label with the sweet spot mark. A well-rolled, solidly struck putt feels as satisfying as a drive hit on the screws. More important, it usually goes where you want.

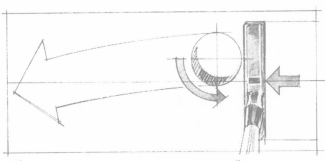

Hitting toward toe imparts "hook-spin."

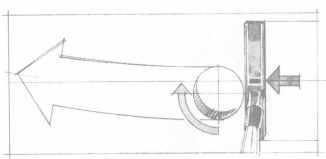

Hitting toward heel imparts "slice-spin."

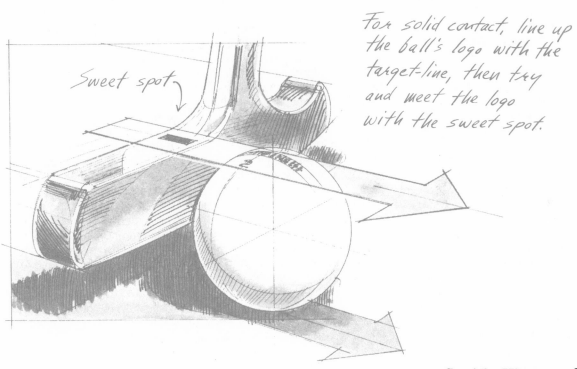

Sweet spot

For solid contact, line up the ball's logo with the target-line, then try and meet the logo with the sweet spot.

8

DRAWS GO FARTHER

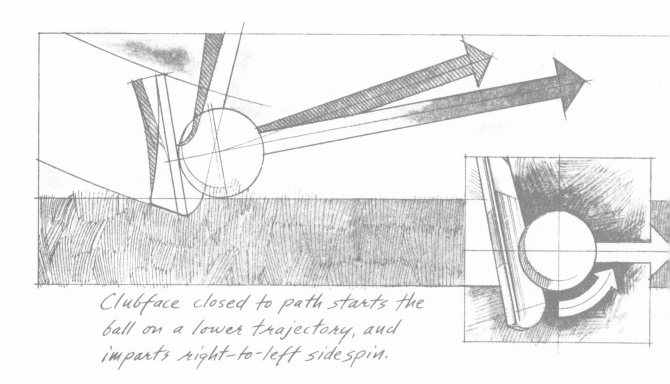

Clubface closed to path starts the ball on a lower trajectory, and imparts right-to-left sidespin.

You'd give anything to hit your shots 10 yards longer. Add that to both your drives and your approaches and you'd reach several more holes in regulation.

You may not have the time or energy to work on building physical strength and you don't want to change your swing either: Despite its shortcomings, it's dependable.

Assuming you hit a straight ball, you can gain substantial distance by adjusting your setup so that the draw becomes your basic shot. If you currently hit a fade, you'll gain even more.

WHY A DRAW GOES FARTHER

When you hit a ball dead straight, at impact your club is moving along the target line with the face exactly perpendicular to that line, so that you're striking the shot with the club's true amount of loft.

To hit the draw, however, the clubface must be slightly closed or turned to the left relative to the path of the club. A closed clubface carries a little less than its true loft. So not only does the club impart right-to-left sidespin, it also launches the ball at a lower angle. So the draw will carry a touch farther than the straight shot, as well as gain added roll after it lands.

DRAW WITH YOUR SETUP

Ordinarily, you'd align your body so that lines across your shoulders, hips and toes run parallel to the target line. Instead, align yourself so that these same lines point either directly at your target or a touch to the right of it, depending on how much draw you want.

While lining up your body a little right, remember to set the clubface squarely at the target. Then swing normally along your body line. The clubface will be closed rel-

ative to that line at impact, imparting sidespin so that the ball starts on your body line but draws left, finishing on the target.

If you currently fade or slice the ball, you'll need to make a bigger adjustment in your aim since you probably aim left of the target. As you adjust your body, however, be sure to keep the clubhead facing the target so you get the necessary right-to-left sidespin.

One other tip to enhance a draw: Move the ball back in your stance an inch or two. This ensures that the clubhead path points to the right of the target line at the moment of impact.

Practice until you're accustomed to the new setup and can marry it to your normal swing. Take note of the changes in total distance your shots travel with each club so that you can plan for added distance.

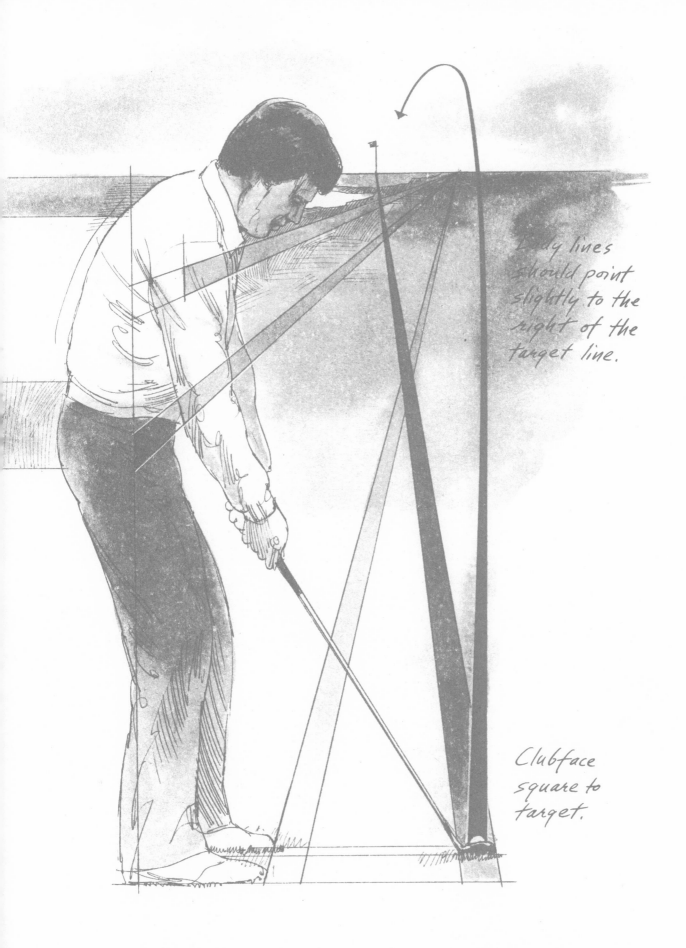

Body lines should point slightly to the right of the target line.

Clubface square to target.

9

BUILD A STRONG LEFT SIDE

Golf is a two-sided game, yet many shorter hitters rely on their right sides to push the club through the swing while keeping the weaker left side quiet. Building up strength in a relatively passive port side will increase clubhead speed for extra distance. Limber up your left side and add length to your shots with these two exercise drills.

DOOR-FRAME PULL
This isometric exercise is simple to do and especially good indoors.

Door Frame Drill - To strengthen the pulling muscles of the left side, take your address position with the clubface flush against the bottom of the doorframe, and pull your hands toward your imaginary target, keeping the left side firm.

Grip a 5-iron, press the face against the bottom of a doorframe and take your address position. Move into what feels like the ideal impact position—knees flexed, weight mostly on your left foot, shoulders square and head down. Keeping your left arm straight and firm, pull the club against the doorframe with the left side using as much force as possible while keeping the right side passive. Hold this position for five seconds and relax. Repeat 20 times. Not only will this exercise help stretch and strengthen key muscles in the left side, it also will build "muscle memory" of the correct impact position.

TIRE DRILL

Tour players hit down on the ball on their iron shots and usually take a divot. But your irons usually bounce off the ground because you lack the strength in your hands, especially the left, to drive the clubface down into the back of the ball.

The great British champion Henry Cotton prescribed the "Tire Drill" for building strength in the left hand and wrist. Lay an old automobile tire flat on the ground. Holding a straight-faced club, such as a 3-iron, with the left hand alone, "address" the tire as you would a ball. Try to smack the clubface flush into the tire. Grip tightly and keep at it for about five minutes or until your hand and forearm are tired. A few minutes a day of this exercise will do wonders for your iron play after a few weeks.

Tire Drill— Good hand strength is needed to hit crisp iron shots. Build power in your left side and hand by smacking a tire with an iron using the left arm alone.

10

STOP PLAYING BASEBALL GOLF

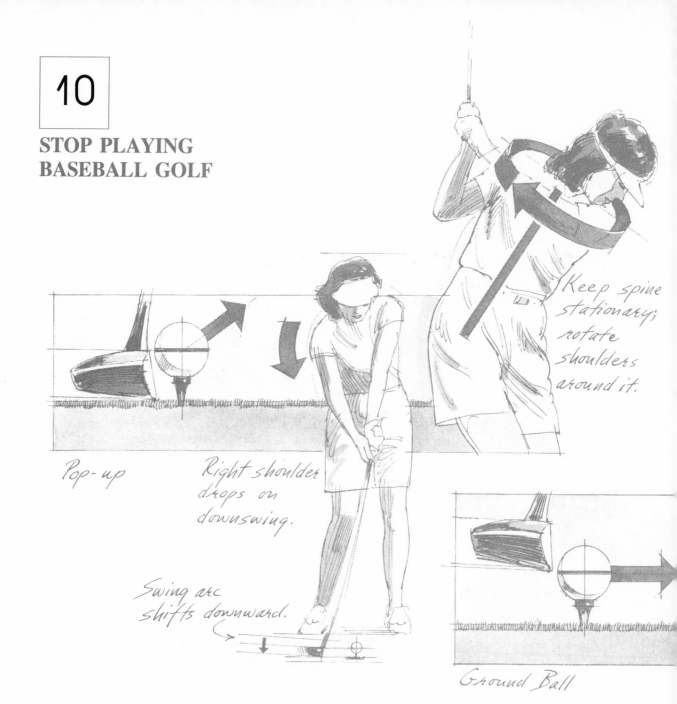

Pop-up

Right shoulder drops on downswing.

Swing arc shifts downward.

Keep spine stationary; rotate shoulders around it.

Ground Ball

To get the maximum distance from your swing, you must put the clubface squarely on the ball. Since shorter hitters don't generate a lot of clubhead speed, they can't afford less than solid contact. Unfortunately, in trying for more distance off the tee, many swing too hard and end up playing "baseball golf"—hitting mainly pop-ups and grounders that don't go nearly as far as a well-struck shot.

POP-UPS: PREVENT THE RIGHT SHOULDER-DROP

A pop-up or "skyed" tee shot occurs when the top edge of the clubface makes contact below the ball's equator. The ball then rockets very high but not very far. The poor contact is the result of the right shoulder dropping during the downswing, causing a lowering of the swing arc, which allows the clubhead to sweep under the ball instead of flush into it. Ironically, the shoulder drops when the player tries to generate more power and lunges at the ball.

To prevent the right shoulder-drop and keep the level of your swing consistent, try the following: 1) Keep your weight off your toes at address. 2) Hover the club-head gently in the grass rather than pushing down in it. 3) On the backswing, keep your spine stationary while rotating your shoulders around it, then shift your weight from the right side to the left to start the downswing and unwind your shoulders around the spine, which remains fixed. 4) Don't think about your hands, arms or even hitting the ball: Think only about turning your shoulders smoothly and quickly.

GROUNDERS: THE HIPS STAY LEVEL

A grounder off the tee can be more harmful than a pop-up: At least the high-flyer has a chance of

Make sure your right hip stays level with your left.

Straightening right leg causes right hip to rise.

Swing arc shifts upward.

Drill 1: Stop Popping Up Practice swinging an old driver while standing on a hard surface, like your driveway. To avoid banging the clubhead into the pavement, you'll automatically learn to keep the right shoulder from dropping.

Drill 2: An End to Ground Balls Stick a tee in the ground so it stands straight, but don't put a ball on it. Swing your driver trying to uproot the tee and knock it down the fairway. Do this 100 times, then tee up a ball and watch it fly.

sailing over trouble in front of the tee. The "worm-burner" occurs when the bottom edge of the club-face hits above the ball's equator. Like the pop-up, the grounder usually follows an attempt at building power. In this instance, in trying to activate the lower body, the right leg straightens on the downswing, raising the right hip and the swing arc.

To prevent grounders: 1) At address, keep your weight off your heels. 2) Flex your knees. 3) On the downswing, remember to keep the right hip level with the left: *Turn* the hips, don't tilt them.

11

HOME IMPROVEMENT

Keep the feeling of contact fresh by putting a few balls on a rug.

If you've already put the sticks in storage, take them out. You can keep your swing oiled and your touch sharp during a long, cold winter. In fact, the off-season can be a great time to work on grooving a good swing, strengthening the golf muscles and curing a nagging fault.

STAY "IN TOUCH" WITH THE BALL

Touch or feel takes time to develop and is quickly lost; you can keep a sharp finesse game during the winter layoff with a little indoor practice. Spend a few minutes a day chipping and putting on a rug, but don't overdo it: You're trying to keep fresh the feeling of crisp club-to-ball contact. A few minutes' practice may not seem like much, but when you head out after the first thaw this spring, it will have made a difference.

SWING A HEAVY CLUB

Making practice swings in your garage may not be your idea of fun, but it's better for your swing than sitting around the house for three or four months. You don't want your body to forget the feel of a good swing.

Spend 10 minutes a day swinging a heavy club, an exercise that encourages a number of good swing moves. The additional weight forces you to make a one-piece takeaway, which leads to a good shoulder turn. It also helps eliminate any abrupt actions that can wreck proper timing: Besides the slow, even takeaway, feel a smooth transition between the end of the backswing and the start of the downswing.

On the downswing, the heavy club forces you to accelerate through the hitting zone and release your hands properly. You'll also be building up the muscles you use in swinging the club.

FIXING FAULTS

Winter is a fine time to practice keeping your head still during the swing. (Many golfers report that their first rounds of golf in the spring are replete with mishits caused by a wandering head.) Use your winter practice swings to concentrate on keeping the head relatively still.

Similarly, devote the cold-weather layoff to building up your hip turn or making a better weight shift. Whatever needs work, the off-season is a good time to make repairs and improvements.

Drill: Swing a weighted club
Start with just a little extra weight to prevent straining any muscles, and add weight as you feel more comfortable. Don't try to dominate it— swing it smoothly and easily. Your swing path, hand action, strength and tempo will improve for it.

12

CHECK FOR POWER LEAKS

Shoulders rotate around spine while left arm and wrist remain firm

← Knees flexed

Weight toward balls of feet

Power leaks are flaws that keep you from creating maximum club-head speed. Plug these leaks to get more distance on your shots.

THE QUICK PICKUP
Picking up the clubhead quickly on the takeaway leads to numerous power leaks. First, it shrinks the size of the swing arc. Second, it usually limits the shoulder turn and creates an arms-only swing, a weak pass at the ball.

Don't think "hands" on the take-away but concentrate on turning the shoulders around your spine, keeping the left arm and wrist firm as the club moves away from the ball.

POOR WEIGHT WORK
At the top of the backswing, your right knee should be flexed and your weight on the inside of the right foot. Many shorter hitters allow their weight to roll to the out-side of the right foot; it restricts the coil of the hips and shoulders and leads to swaying off the ball.

The best way to get the weight on the inside of the right foot is to key on turning the hips in the back-

swing rather than letting them slide to the right.

STAY OFF YOUR HEELS
A common fault among shorter hitters is letting the weight fall back on their heels as they start the downswing, which leads to a powerless swing. The problem usually begins with poor posture at address. Make sure your knees are flexed and the weight is on the balls

of your feet. Maintain your knee flex through the backswing, then slide your knees aggressively toward the target—not back toward your heels—on the down-swing. Think of driving your lower body toward the left leg, which stays flexed but firm to handle the load. The force of the lower body moving toward the target will help pull the club down and through the ball with power.

Coiled for power

Knees flexed

Turn shoulders and hips into a braced right leg.

Weight on inside of right foot

Slide your knees aggressively toward the target.

13

MAKE TWO—OR BETTER—LONG PUTTS

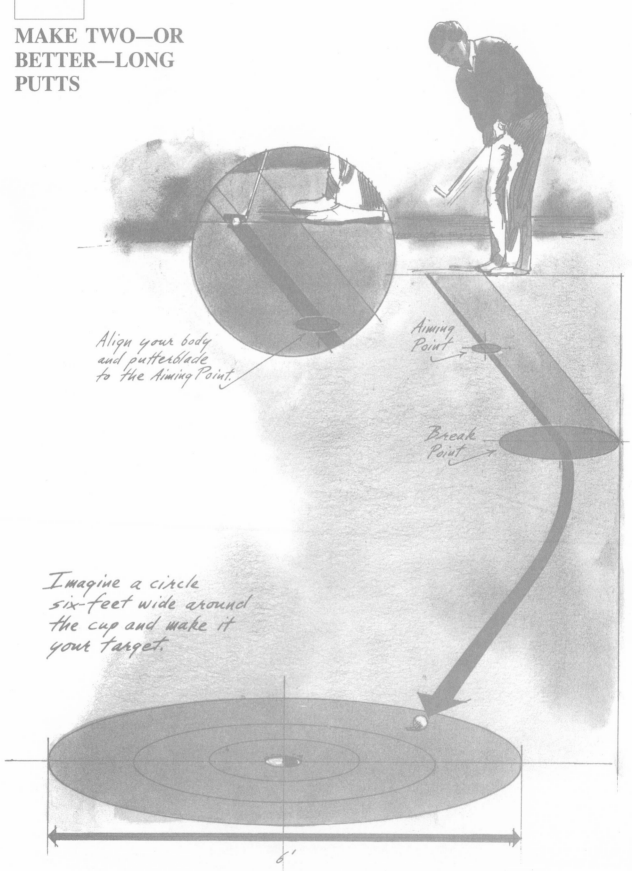

Align your body and putterblade to the Aiming Point.

Aiming Point

Break Point

Imagine a circle six-feet wide around the cup and make it your target.

6'

On very long putts, a smooth arm-and-shoulder stroke works best.

You approach many greens with fairway woods and long irons, so probably you face a good number of long putts per round. The more often you can get down in two (or even one) from three-putt territory, the more strokes you'll save.

PUTT DEFENSIVELY
Start by considering your strategy. If you consistently are taking three putts from long range, you might be trying too hard to sink the first one.

On a 40-foot chip, you're satisfied to get close enough for a tap in. So why do you try to hole a 70-foot putt? Even pros are happy with a two-putt on very long ones and consider themselves lucky when the first one drops. Your objective should be the same: Get the ball close to the hole with your first putt and safely in the cup in two.

One of the oldest tricks to get the first putt close is to aim for an imaginary circle six-feet wide around the cup. If the ball finishes inside it, you have a makeable three footer or less. You'll soon find that the better you get at lagging the ball into the big circle, the more often the ball will find the small one.

AIM AT A SPOT, NOT THE HOLE
Choose a spot along the line of your putt and aim for it, not the hole. Pick a mark on the surface—an old ball mark or dead spot will do, the closer to you, the better.

On long, sloping putts, pick out the break point, where you think the putt will begin to curve. Aim for that, aligning your putter-blade and body to it.

MAKE A LONG, SMOOTH STROKE
On long putts, make a long, smooth, arm-and-shoulder stroke. Use the big muscles of the body—such as the shoulders and arms—rather than the little muscles of a wristy stroke.

Wristiness can cause you to lift the putterhead going back, so you hit down or up on the ball instead of accelerating through it. It's difficult to control pace when the wrists do the putting.

Remember that the putting stroke actually is a small version of your big swing, so rhythm and tempo are important for rolling the ball over long distances. Concentrate on taking the putter back slowly and smoothly, then pulling it through the ball with a fluid motion, making solid contact without trying to steer the shot.

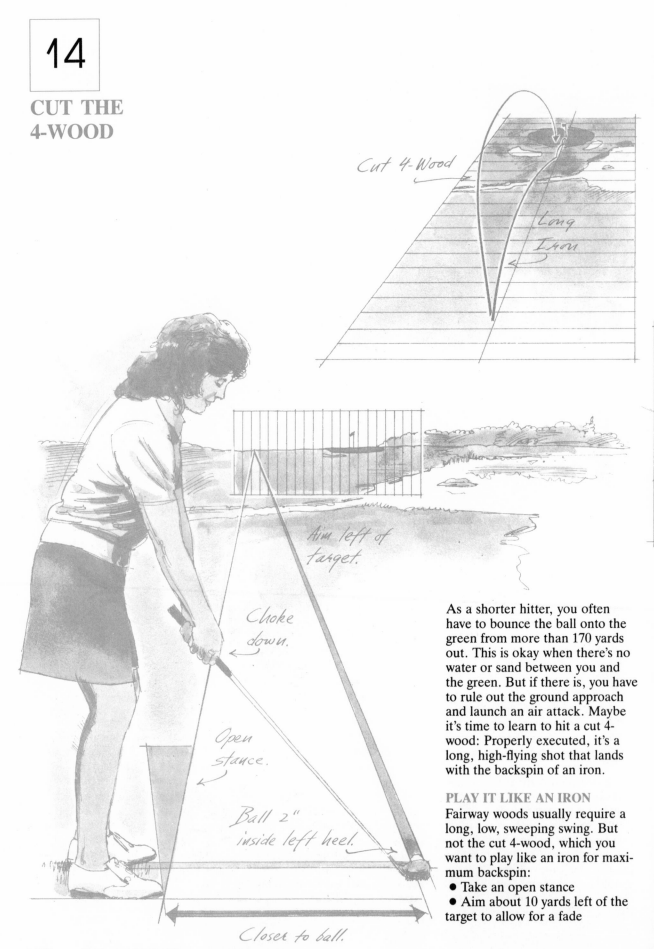

14

CUT THE 4-WOOD

Cut 4-Wood

Long Iron

Aim left of target.

Choke down.

Open stance.

Ball 2" inside left heel.

Closer to ball.

As a shorter hitter, you often have to bounce the ball onto the green from more than 170 yards out. This is okay when there's no water or sand between you and the green. But if there is, you have to rule out the ground approach and launch an air attack. Maybe it's time to learn to hit a cut 4-wood: Properly executed, it's a long, high-flying shot that lands with the backspin of an iron.

PLAY IT LIKE AN IRON

Fairway woods usually require a long, low, sweeping swing. But not the cut 4-wood, which you want to play like an iron for maximum backspin:
● Take an open stance
● Aim about 10 yards left of the target to allow for a fade

The shot will fly high and stop quickly

Ball struck first, with descending blow.

- Choke down an inch
- Stand an inch closer to the ball
- Play the ball two inches behind the left heel.

These adjustments will result in a more upright swing and more descending blow. You should hit the ball before the ground, perhaps even taking a divot. The shot will fly high and stop quickly upon landing. Because it's a fade, it's easier to control.

You won't get your usual distance with the 4-wood. Count on losing 10-15 yards.

If you hit this shot into wind, expect it to fly much higher—and shorter—than usual. Also, the wind will exaggerate the fade.

Try the same technique with the 5-wood for shorter cut shots.

STRATEGY FOR
LONG PAR FOURS

If you can't reach in two, play smart and pick out an area in front of the green that will offer the best angle to make a good pitch.

Try to place your ball in the position where you'll have the simplest putt for par.

Because power is not your game, many of the longer par fours, ranging from about 420 to 470 yards, fall outside your reach in two. You still can bag your fair share of pars on the very long ones if you follow an intelligent strategy for playing them.

PLAY FOR FIVE
Start by judging your abilities fairly. On a hole this long, five is a good score for you, so treat it as a par five.

You likely know deep down that hitting the green in two is beyond your game. But standing over a 3-wood shot, the temptation is there that if you swing a little harder and get it all…. The usual result is a mishit, leaving a tough third shot to the green and a struggle to make bogey.

Be honest about your talent: Not distance but accuracy is your strength. If you can't reach the green in two, play smart and pick out an area in front of the green that will offer the best angle to make a good pitch to the pin, without any hazards and leaving you with an opening to shoot at plenty of green.

That doesn't necessarily mean hitting a 3-wood as far as you can. Depending on the situation, you may want to take less club and lay up to allow yourself a full shot into the green, or to put yourself on a level part of the fairway instead of a sloping lie. Make it your goal to put the ball in the spot that sets up the easiest pitch or chip.

KEEP SHORT GAME SHARP
The true test will be the third shot, since the pars you make depend on your short game. The better you are at getting up and down, the more pars you'll walk away with, so develop a good short game.

Getting up and down is more than being able to hit shots. You must study the green, noticing its contours. You'll probably want to place the ball below the cup, leaving a fairly straight, short uphill putt.

You'll find that planning this strategy before teeing off will boost your confidence, another key ingredient to turning those bogey fives into par fours.

16

STAY BEHIND THE BALL

Head behind ball at address.

Imagine a straight line between the ball and your left ear.

Shift lower body.

Head behind ball.

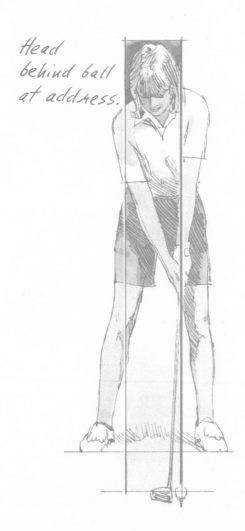

To add distance to their shots, players often are advised to make the lower body more active as a way of putting power into the downswing. But it's easy to overdo leg and hip action, which usually results in upper body movement toward the target as well. What usually follows is either a badly pulled shot or a pull slice.

"Staying behind" the ball helps you swing down freely with your hands and arms while keeping the lower body from getting out of control. It also encourages your hands to release through the ball, resulting in a distance-producing draw.

KEEP YOUR HEAD BACK

Though it may sound contradictory, you have to keep your upper body stationary while shifting your lower body toward the target on the downswing. But there is an excellent swing key to help you do this.

If you position the ball correctly with your driver, it should be anywhere between the left heel and instep. With the ball there, you should have no trouble imagining that your head is *behind* the ball at address. The key, then, is to concentrate on shifting your lower body toward the target on the downswing while keeping your head behind the ball. You should

feel as if your hands are swinging freely past your chin at impact and well beyond it as you keep your head still and extend your arms toward the target. Try to keep your head down until the momentum of the follow-through pulls it and your body up into the finish position.

OR, DON'T CROSS THE LINE

Another key to use to keep the upper body behind the ball is to imagine a line running straight up and down between the ball and your left ear. Now swing, keeping your ear behind the line. Again, keep it back until the force of the swing brings your head up.

Head should stay still until the momentum of the follow-through pulls it up.

17

GET A LONGER DRIVER

A longer driver guarantees greater clubhead speed.

More flexible shaft makes it easier to get height and right-to-left flight for distance.

You may not be as short a driver as you think. It's possible—even likely—that the club you're using is costing you yardage.

You know you're not a power player who can pound a drive 275 yards. You should also understand that certain equipment characteristics, which might not apply to other golfers, will help you hit the ball farther.

Let's take a look at several areas of golf club design that can help you, the relatively short hitter, to gain more distance.

1. *Longer shafts*. Simple physics tells you that the farther the clubhead travels, the more speed it will develop by impact. You may be able to swing a driver slightly longer than the standard 43 inches—say, one-half-inch to an inch longer—without sacrificing accuracy. Of course, first check if your build allows you to swing a longer club comfortably. The best way is to have a pro measure the distance from your fingertips to the ground while you stand erect. If this distance is longer than nor-

mal, he might advise longer clubs. Another clue is to check your shirt sleeve length. Is it shorter than normal for a person your height? This implies that you can use a longer club.

Remember that the longer the club, the more you will swing it around and behind you. So you'll tend to hit the ball lower and with a draw.

2. *Shallower clubface/greater loft*. Because you don't generate a lot of clubhead speed, a driver with only average loft may cause shots

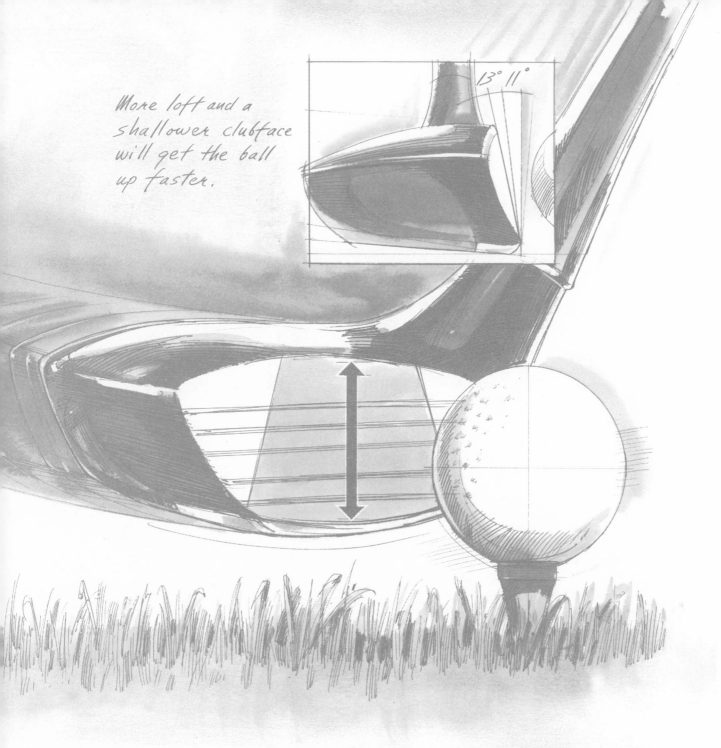

More loft and a shallower clubface will get the ball up faster.

13° 11°

that nosedive early. You need to keep the ball in the air longer to achieve maximum distance. This means using more loft than average on your driving club and possibly using a shallower clubface as well.

A club with some extra loft, say, 13 degrees instead of 11, will launch the ball higher. Also, the shallower the face, the more the clubhead's mass will contact the ball below its equator, getting it to fly higher.

Some straight hitters would actually hit longer tee shots by forgetting the driver entirely and hitting a 2- or 3-wood instead. One of these clubs will provide the optimum launch angle, given the speed generated at impact. Don't hesitate to switch to a 2- or 3-wood if it gives you a better trajectory and more distance.

3. *Whippier shafts.* If your shots fly low, short and tend to fade, a more flexible shaft can give you an automatic distance boost. The added flex means that at impact the club will be bowed so the clubface is ahead of the shaft and the head contacts the ball with added loft. The clubface also is working into a more closed position, making it easier to draw the ball, which automatically gives you a few extra yards.

You'll benefit by using a regular or flexible shaft if you aren't already, but there is a range of flexes within these categories. Hit some practice shots using various shaft flexes until you find the club that gives maximum loft and distance without sacrificing control.

Straight Hitter 119

18

TURN, DON'T TILT

Shoulders tilted

Left arm bent

Weak body coil

When you tilt, clubhead speed is generated mainly from arms and hands.

Many shorter hitters have an extra 15 to 20 yards hidden in their swings. This distance remains untapped because these golfers tilt their shoulders on the back-swing instead of turning them. A correct turn, with your front shoulder coming under your chin, stores power like a coiling spring. If you tilt—turning your shoulders just a bit, then moving the club up with the arms— whatever clubhead speed you generate comes mainly from your hands and arms, with little contribution from the big muscles in the torso or legs. And you need action from those big muscles for distance.

KEEP THE LEFT ARM FIRM
One cause of a tilt is letting the left arm bend on the backswing. A big left-arm break creates only the illusion of a good, full backswing when in fact there is no coil. Firm your left arm and learn to get the club in the same position at the top by turning your shoulders.

SET UP FOR A TURN
Another way to encourage a good turn rather than a powerless tilt is to set up with the shoulders in the proper position. The shoulders start square to the target line, the right a little lower than the left. Your back should be straight so shoulders and hips can revolve easily around the axis of the spine. Your chin should be off your chest to allow full freedom of move-ment. Remember, you want the front shoulder to rotate under the chin, so your head must be up to accommodate it.

MINIMIZE WRISTINESS
A wristy swing also promotes a tilt. You're supposed to rely on the shoulders to get to the top. An early wrist break brings the club behind your head without the shoulders doing much work. Keep hands and wrists quiet but not stiff and start the takeaway by moving the left shoulder toward your chin. The wrists will hinge automatically about waist height and be fully cocked at the top.

CHOOSE YOUR KEY
Besides changing swing mechan-ics, you can help eliminate tilting and initiate a good turn by con-centrating on a positive swing thought. Any of these should help: Turn the left shoulder back to the position of the right shoulder at address; turn your back until it faces the target; turn your chest so it faces away from the target; pull the right shoulder up, around and toward the target.

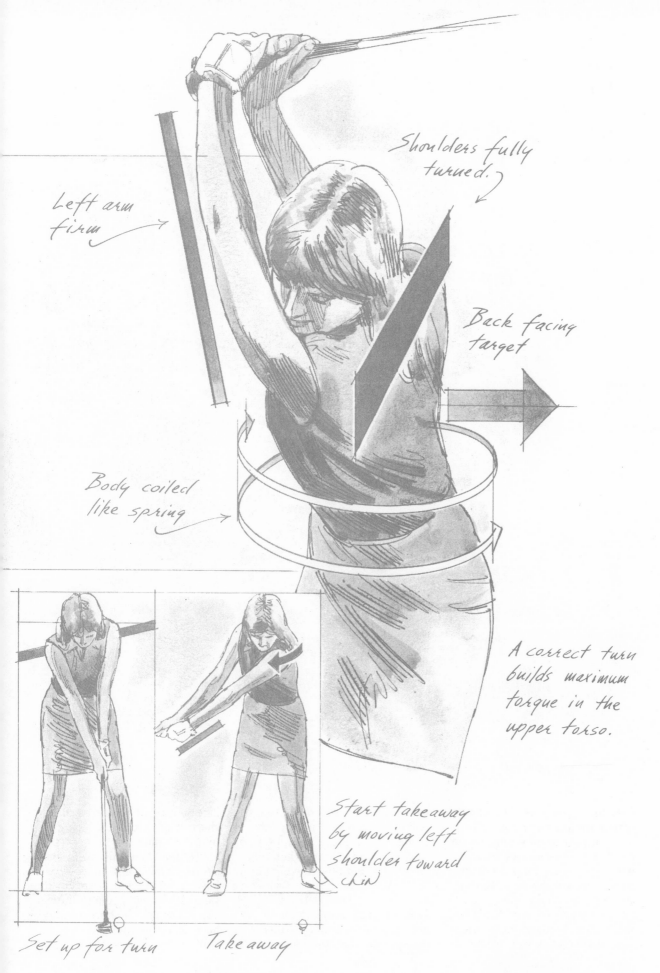

Left arm firm

Shoulders fully turned.

Back facing target

Body coiled like spring

A correct turn builds maximum torque in the upper torso.

Start takeaway by moving left shoulder toward chin

Set up for turn

Take away

19

THE WOOD FROM A FAIRWAY TRAP

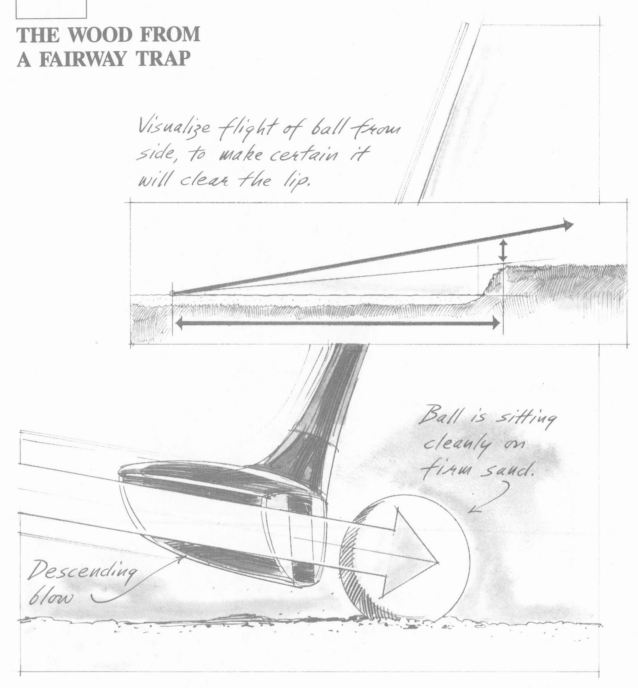

Visualize flight of ball from side, to make certain it will clear the lip.

Ball is sitting cleanly on firm sand.

Descending blow

One thing you know you can't expect to do on the course is fly the ball past fairway bunkers on par fours. On those occasions when your drive finds a fairway trap, you probably assume that you have no choice but to reach for your wedge or 9-iron, play out safely and try to get on in three.

Sometimes this will be the case, but there are other times when you can save a stroke by going for the green with a lofted fairway wood. Here's when you should try and how to go about it.

GOOD LIE, LOW LIP

Lofted fairway woods (5-, 6- or 7-) are ideal from fairway bunkers because they get the ball into the air quickly and don't have an iron's sharp leading edge, which digs into the sand.

Use the wood only if the ball is sitting cleanly on firm sand; you have to hit the ball first, not the sand. If the ball is plugged or in a cuppy lie, take a short iron and hit it as far as you can.

From the side of the trap,

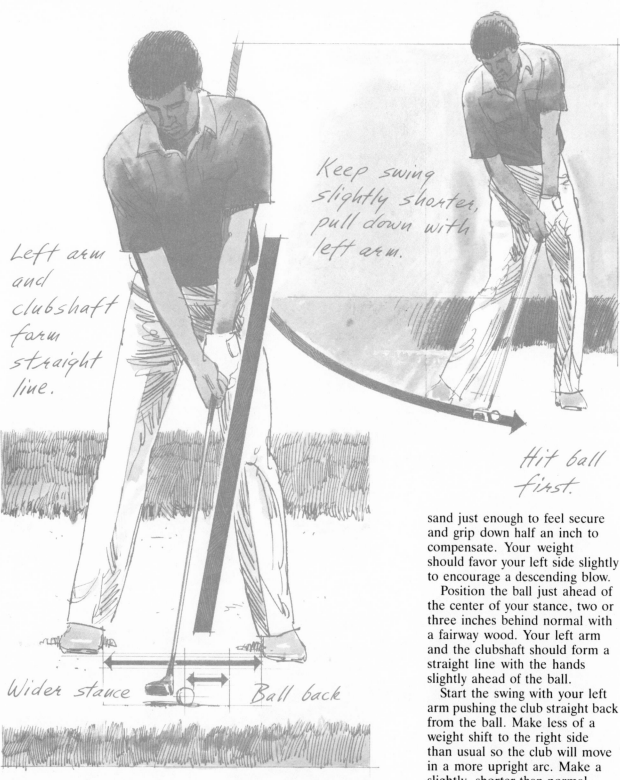

Left arm and clubshaft form straight line.

Keep swing slightly shorter, pull down with left arm.

Hit ball first.

Wider stance

Ball back

check the height of the front lip to estimate the starting trajectory of the shot necessary to clear the lip. Most fairway traps are shallow, so unless the ball is close to the lip getting out shouldn't be a problem. But you'll be hitting with a more descending blow than usual, so the ball will start a little lower, and this must be taken into account.

WIDER BASE, BALL BACK
The key to a successful shot is hitting the ball before hitting the sand. Widen your stance by about two inches to create a stable base that will keep you from moving off the ball during the backswing. Dig your feet into the sand just enough to feel secure and grip down half an inch to compensate. Your weight should favor your left side slightly to encourage a descending blow.

Position the ball just ahead of the center of your stance, two or three inches behind normal with a fairway wood. Your left arm and the clubshaft should form a straight line with the hands slightly ahead of the ball.

Start the swing with your left arm pushing the club straight back from the ball. Make less of a weight shift to the right side than usual so the club will move in a more upright arc. Make a slightly shorter-than-normal swing for balance and control, then pull down with your left arm and hit the ball first (concentrating on the top part of the ball might help you avoid hitting "fat"). Extend your arms straight toward the target after impact.

Don't be afraid to reach for a lofted wood when the conditions are right. You just might reach the green.

20

FINISH YOUR SWING

Your image should be of finishing with the hands high... belt buckle facing the target.

Complete the circle for a good follow-through.

You strike the ball solidly enough, but seldom experience the thrill of a long shot. Your grip, setup and swing feel correct, but something is missing. A common problem among shorter-hitting golfers is the failure to complete the downswing. That is, they actually decelerate into the hitting zone, resulting in an abbreviated follow-through and a weak hit. By learning to finish your swing with a full follow-through, you'll add needed clubhead speed, which results in additional distance on your shots.

THINK "THROUGH," NOT "TO"
Many golfers become so "ball conscious" that once they sense impact, they consider the swing over and stop. In essence, they are playing little more than a punch shot and are sacrificing distance for it. To add length to your long shots, think of swinging through the ball, not to the ball. Visualize a post-swing position that indicates a full, free downswing and then attempt to actually create that image with a practice swing. A common position that indicates a full finish is that of

having your belt-buckle facing the target at the completion of the swing, with your hands high over your left shoulder.

A FULL CIRCLE SWING
Think of the swing as a circle, with the ball nothing more than a point on it that falls in the path of the clubface. In practice, attempt to swing in a complete circle. The hands swing back to a point over your shoulders at the top of the backswing, so to complete the circle, they must finish very near that point in the follow-through.

Start-at-the-Top-Drill

Assume a three-quarter backswing position and start the downswing from there to get the feel of accelerating through the impact zone and into a full follow-through. This drill forces you to swing with your hands and arms — just a few minutes of it will have you finishing high.

21

THE LOW
RUN-UP

Pick a spot several feet onto the green, then use the club that will land the ball there and let it run to the hole.

If you keep the ball in play but have trouble reaching the greens in regulation, you'll probably face more than your share of 20- to 30-yard shots from right in front. Though these shots usually are open, judging distance is a perpetual problem, especially when the pin is in back or on a second tier. If you automatically reach for a wedge on these shots, put it away and play the mid-iron run-up instead.

LAND IT ON, LET IT RUN
Mechanics matter less than visualization when you're trying to get this shot close. Address the ball with a narrow, open stance and with your hands in front of the clubface to help you make a descending blow. Swing the club back and through with your arms, keeping your wrists firm; this way you fight the tendency to lift or scoop at the ball with the clubface.

Always try to land the ball just on the putting surface so it runs the distance to the hole. It's easier to judge the distance the ball will roll than its flight. Since you're not trying to get the ball high, you can use a 6-, 7- or 8-iron; your contact will be more consistently solid with a straighter-faced club than with a wedge.

Pick a spot that's at least four to five feet onto the green, then concentrate on landing the ball right on that spot. Even if you make a slight error in execution, the ball will still land on the green.

If you're a few feet off the green so you need very little carry on the ball, you might find the 6-iron the right choice for your run-up. If you're five yards off, the 7-iron might be the club. If you're six to eight yards off, you'll need a bit more carry so the 8-iron might provide the right combination of loft and roll. It will take a little practice to find the right club for each situation, but if you adhere to the "run-up" principle whenever you can use it, you'll consistently get these short shots to finish close to the hole. ■

Low Handicapper

You have a sound all-around game, but you'd like to shave those last few strokes off your handicap.

The golfer who regularly shoots in the 70s and low 80s is one of the stars of his club. He is a trend-setter, a player whom others look up to and seek advice from on everything from technique to equipment. But the good player also is a smart player, one who knows that his game can stand some improvement.

Obviously the low-handicap golfer doesn't require much help with swing mechanics; he hasn't reached this level by making a poor pass at the ball (or if he has, he won't remain a low handicapper for long). Similarly, he can hit most of the shots. But even pros know that strokes can be saved in the short game and on the greens, so these areas receive attention in this chapter.

Where good golfers can use the most help is upstairs, between the ears. At this level it's mental preparation that makes the difference between an okay round and a great one. Therefore, most of the articles in this section deal with strategy, particularly in competition, and course management. Also offered are advanced techniques, including a few unusual shots that will bail out a sticky situation and, executed successfully, raise the low handicapper's already high profile.

1

HOW TO PREPARE FOR A TOURNAMENT

Like many good players, you enjoy playing in tournaments and you play to win. To be successful in competition requires a knowledge of the course and those parts of your game that will help you beat it.

Do some pacing and make a yardage book.

Put some extra time in practicing the specific areas the course will demand.

KNOW THE COURSE

Playing on your home course eases your homework for the obvious reason: You already know the layout very well. Even so, spend some time running through the course in your head and develop a game plan. Don't simply rely on familiarity to breed success.

If the tournament is over unfamiliar ground, play a practice round and check it out. Is the course short and tight with a premium on accuracy, or long and open favoring distance? Can you play it aggressively and still save par if a shot goes astray? Are there many hazards to penalize a bad shot?

What kind of approach shots does the course demand? Will you be hitting middle irons or short irons into the greens? Can you hit the par fives in two with your fairway woods or are you better off laying off and concentrating on wedging the ball close for possible birdies? The placement of the hazards will have a lot to do with that.

How are the greens? Slick ones require a delicate touch, so you might switch to a lighter putter. On slow greens, a heavier putter might help. Make a yardage book by pacing off par-four and par-five holes. It will give you confidence when selecting a club during the tournament.

PREPARE YOUR GAME

Once you have a good idea what the course calls for, go to the practice area and sharpen those parts of your game. For example, spend time in the practice bunker if the course features a lot of sand. If your tee shots have been wild and the course is narrow, work on straightening them out or experiment with safer clubs off the tee. If you'll be hitting a lot of long irons, make sure you have confidence in them.

START EARLY

Don't wait until the day before the tournament to hit the practice tee. Start your preparation early. Learn what the course is like, its lengths and its hazards. Practice those parts of your game you'll need the most.

The confidence you build by having done your homework will let you play your best during competition. Good luck!

2

WHEN YOU'RE "IN BETWEEN" CLUBS

Choke down

Choking down decreases the size of your swing arc.

Normal arc

Smaller arc

Being caught "in between" clubs is one of the toughest situations in golf. What do you do when a 7-iron is too much club but an 8-iron is too little? First, the nagging indecision probably won't allow you to concentrate on the shot. Second, either you try hitting a "soft" 7, let up on it and miss the shot, or you try jumping on the 8-iron and flub it. The next time you're in between clubs, try one of these methods.

CHOKE DOWN ON THE LONGER CLUB
Take the longer of the two clubs, choke down on the grip about an inch and hit a normal shot. Choking down shrinks the size of the swing arc, which cuts the speed of the clubhead and the distance the ball flies.

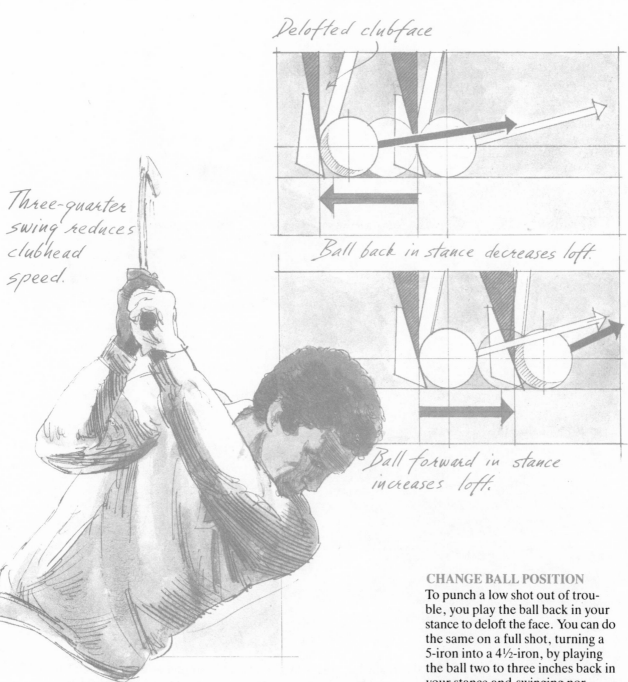

Three-quarter swing reduces clubhead speed.

Delofted clubface

Ball back in stance decreases loft.

Ball forward in stance increases loft.

MAKE A THREE-QUARTER SWING

Swinging the longer club less than all the way back reduces clubhead speed through impact, making the shot shorter. As a low handicapper, you should be comfortable hitting less-than-full wedge shots: Imagine the feel of a three-quarter wedge when trying to hit another club, whether you're swinging a 3-wood or an 8-iron.

CHANGE BALL POSITION

To punch a low shot out of trouble, you play the ball back in your stance to deloft the face. You can do the same on a full shot, turning a 5-iron into a 4½-iron, by playing the ball two to three inches back in your stance and swinging normally. Play for a left-to-right shot, since the clubface won't square up in time and will be slightly open at impact.

To increase the loft of a club, making the ball fly higher and shorter than usual, play the ball two to three inches forward in your stance. This shot will move from right-to-left since the clubface will be closed at impact.

Practice all these shots before you need them. That way, you'll see how much a change in grip, size of swing or ball position affects distance.

3

PICK THE RIGHT DRIVER

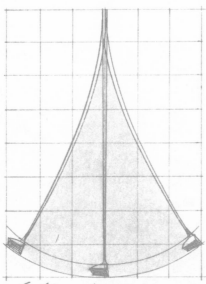

Softer shaft provides more "kick;" stiffer shaft offers strong player greater control.

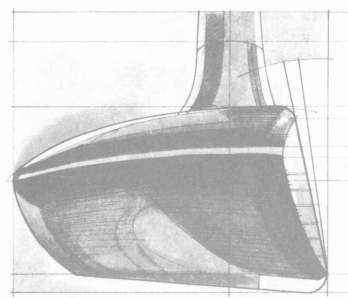

You can easily alter the flight of your drives simply by finding the right loft.

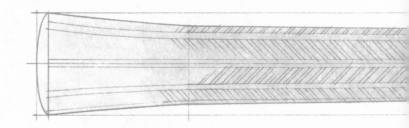

You have a fundamentally sound swing, yet your driving isn't up to your standard. You may be hitting it too high or too low, or bending it more than you want to.

Finding just the right driver for you can be a springboard to low scores. You want a club that complements your swing characteristics so you won't have to worry about making adjustments to get "your" shot. Then you'll be able to swing with more confidence.

It will take time and experimentation to find the right driver for you. You probably won't know exactly what mixture of specifications works best for you until you actually hit balls with a variety of clubs. Here are the areas you should pay close attention to:

SHAFT FLEX
Club manufacturers have advanced beyond producing shafts that are either "regular," "stiff" or "extra stiff." Now you can choose from among several gradations within each range. Chances are you are using a stiff-shafted driver, but you might find that a shaft at the "softer" end of this category provides better feel and more "kick" through impact. Such a shaft will help if you're looking for more distance or are trying to correct a tendency to hit to the right. Conversely, you may want a stiffer shaft if you're hooking the ball or willing to sacrifice distance for control.

CLUBFACE LOFT
Generally speaking, the better player needs less loft since he generates enough clubhead speed to launch the ball with a rising trajectory. Yet, even on the PGA Tour, driver lofts differ widely—from about seven degrees to 12 or more.

Look for a driver with enough loft so you don't have to alter your technique to get the ball up.

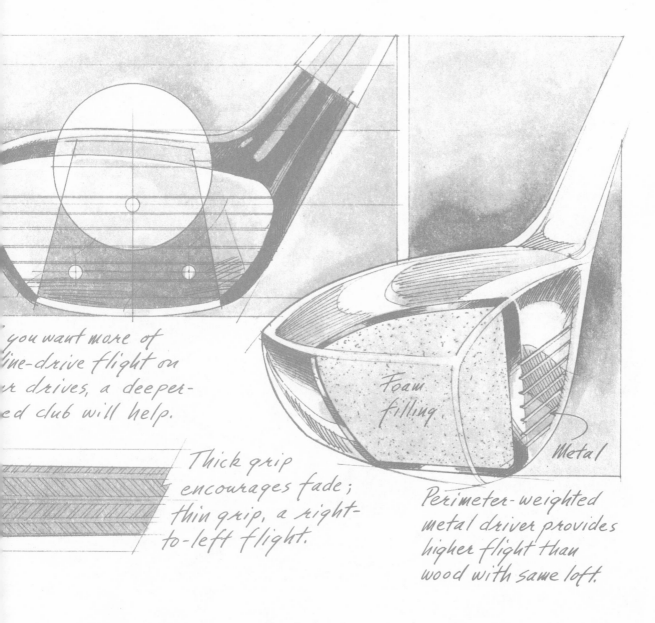

you want more of
line-drive flight on
r drives, a deeper-
ed club will help.

Thick grip
encourages fade;
thin grip, a right-
to-left flight.

Foam
filling

Metal

Perimeter-weighted
metal driver provides
higher flight than
wood with same loft.

But if you can control such a club, stepping down a degree or two will give a more boring flight for more distance and control in wind.

CLUBFACE DEPTH

The deeper the clubface, the lower the ball will fly (assuming the ball is teed at a constant height). That's because as you contact the ball, more of the clubhead's mass will be above the ball's equator at impact, driving the ball down. So if you hit the ball relatively low and want a bit more air time on your tee shots, avoid deep-faced drivers.

GRIP SIZE

The diameter of the grip affects the degree to which your hands and wrists release the clubhead. The thinner the grip, the faster your hands will move and the greater the chances of hitting a draw or hook. A thicker grip tends to slow down wrist action, promoting an open clubface at impact and a left-to-right ball flight.

To test the diameter of your grip, hold the club with your normal left-hand grip. Your third and fourth fingers should be just barely touching the base of your palm.

CLUBHEAD MATERIAL

Wood or metal? It's still a matter of preference since there's no proof that either produces longer or straighter drives. But there are differences in how the two play.

While wood has a consistent density, metal heads are hollow shells with a foam filling. This perimeter weighting, with a higher percentage toward the sole, kicks the ball up in the air faster than wood. Also, metal drivers usually have shallower faces than wood. So, even with identical lofts, a metal driver and a wood model may give very different results.

Low Handicapper 133

4

TWO MIRACLE SHOTS

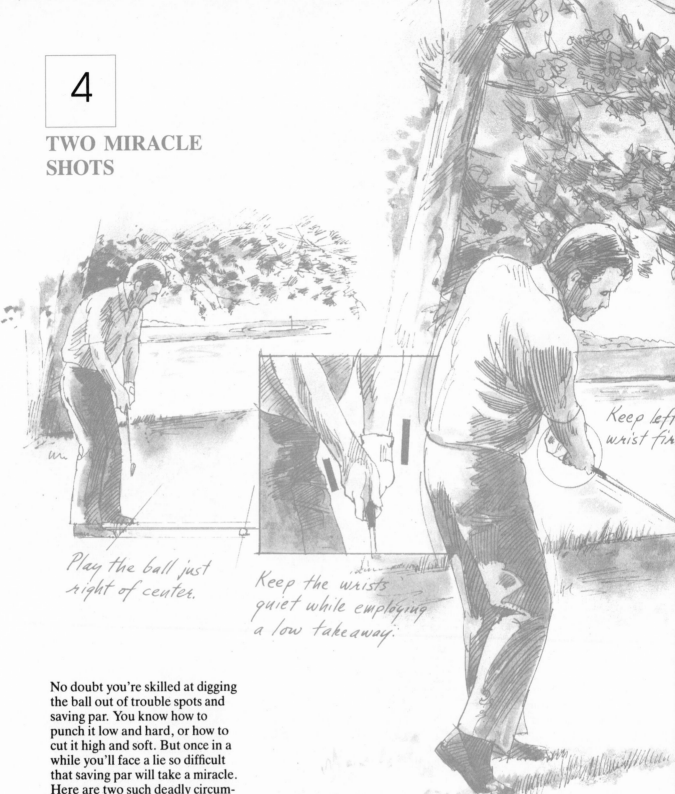

Play the ball just right of center.

Keep the wrists quiet while employing a low takeaway.

Keep left wrist fir...

No doubt you're skilled at digging the ball out of trouble spots and saving par. You know how to punch it low and hard, or how to cut it high and soft. But once in a while you'll face a lie so difficult that saving par will take a miracle. Here are two such deadly circumstances and instructions on the shots necessary to pull them off.

SKIP SHOT

Having driven off line and into trees, you face an approach to a green fronted by a pond. Overhanging branches prevent lofting the ball. Of course, your opponent is safely on the green, forcing you to get down in two. Although highly risky, your only shot is to try skipping the ball off the water and onto the green.

As when skipping a stone, you want the shot to fly low and hard. Take a 3-iron, open the clubface slightly and play the ball off your back foot. Hit down hard, keeping the left wrist firm so the face stays open and puts cutspin on the shot.

Don't let the hands turn over —drawspin will make the ball dive into the drink.

If possible, the ball should hit the water close to the far side so there's less chance of it coming up short. More important: Hit the ball hard! After hitting the water it's unlikely the ball will sail over the green.

RICOCHET SHOT

Your approach has missed the green, the ball coming to rest so close to a tree that you haven't got a backswing. If you must get up and down, turn away from the target and try ricocheting the ball off the tree and onto the green.

Take a club with enough loft that the ball won't rebound straight back and into the clubface. Determine the angle of ricochet necessary to bounce the ball off the trunk and in the general direction. Keep your head and body steady and punch the club sharply into the ball. Swing about twice as hard as you would for a normal shot of that distance. Take care that the ball doesn't fly back and hit you!

On a rebound shot be sure to stay down, maintaining your knee flex, and keep the follow-through short.

5

MASTER THE PAR FIVES

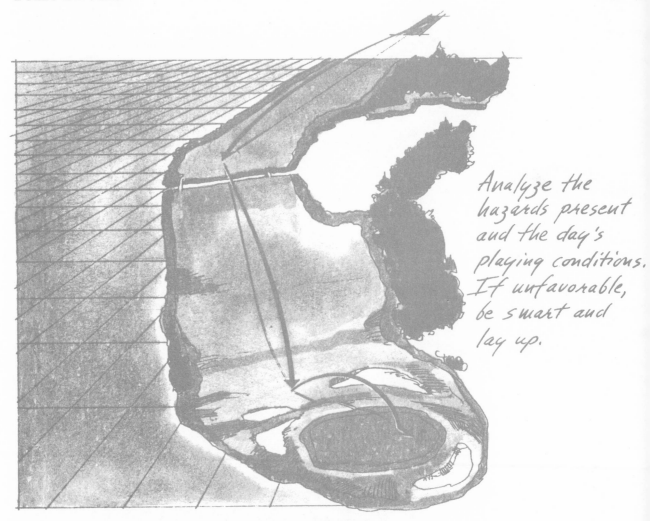

Analyze the hazards present and the day's playing conditions. If unfavorable, be smart and lay up.

Although you consistently score in the 70s, you just can't seem to put it all together for a sub-par round. It could be you're not making enough birdies to bring you into the low numbers. For a player of your caliber, the par fives generally offer the best opportunities to shoot under par. Knowing when to attack and when to play safe will maximize your chances of making birdies (and possibly eagles).

THINK THROUGH THE HOLE
The key to scoring well on any hole is putting the ball into the position that leaves the simplest next shot. Obviously, the simplest third shot on a par five is a putt, but the risks of going for the green in two often outweigh the possible return: The approach probably will be a low percentage wood or long iron shot. Whether you gamble or lay up must be decided by assessing the situation and weighing the possible pluses and minuses. Think your way through the hole before taking any swings.

DETERMINE THE RISKS
Distance is not the only obstacle to getting home on a par five.

Reaching the green in two may be well within your capability, but the margin for error might be slight—and not worth the attempt. Most par fives are designed so that the closer you land the ball to the hazard, the easier your second shot will be.

With this in mind, view the hole as it fits your normal shot shape. For instance, say a pond lies 240 yards out along the left side of the fairway. If your natural shot is a draw, you may want to take a 3-wood and hit away from the trouble. But if you fade the ball, swing away with confidence. Remem-

If you're in the fairway with a possible shot to the green, honestly weigh your chances of making it.

ber, in a pressure situation, go with what's natural.

Carefully consider the penalties of waiting hazards. Though you want to avoid fairway bunkers and rough, you should still be able to salvage par from them. Water and out-of-bounds, however, are a different story; the cost of a stroke or two, and sometimes distance, can turn a near-great round sour in a hurry.

If you determine that the risk is too high, put away the driver, hit away from trouble and don't aim for the green in two. Discretion is an ingredient of good play.

TO GO OR NOT TO GO

Some par fives take two very long, very good shots to have even a chance of getting home. Facing one of these, start by checking the playing conditions on the tee. Is there a headwind that hinders distance; a tailwind to add to it? Is the fairway wet, which reduces roll; or dry, allowing more? Are there any hazards that would make a career drive a disaster?

If you can tell from the tee that there's no way to get home in two this day, then play it safe.

If, however, you go for it and succeed—you're in the fairway

with a possible shot to the green— then start the analysis over again. How severe are the hazards guarding the green? Too many players get excited when in range and fire away without thinking.

Even if the possible pitfalls aren't that severe, honestly weigh your chances of making the shot. Does the situation demand a 220-yard carry over a trap? Is that shot a 1-in-10 chance? If so, be smart and lay up. There's a better chance of getting into birdie range with a wedge from the fairway than from a buried lie in a greenside bunker.

Low Handicapper   137

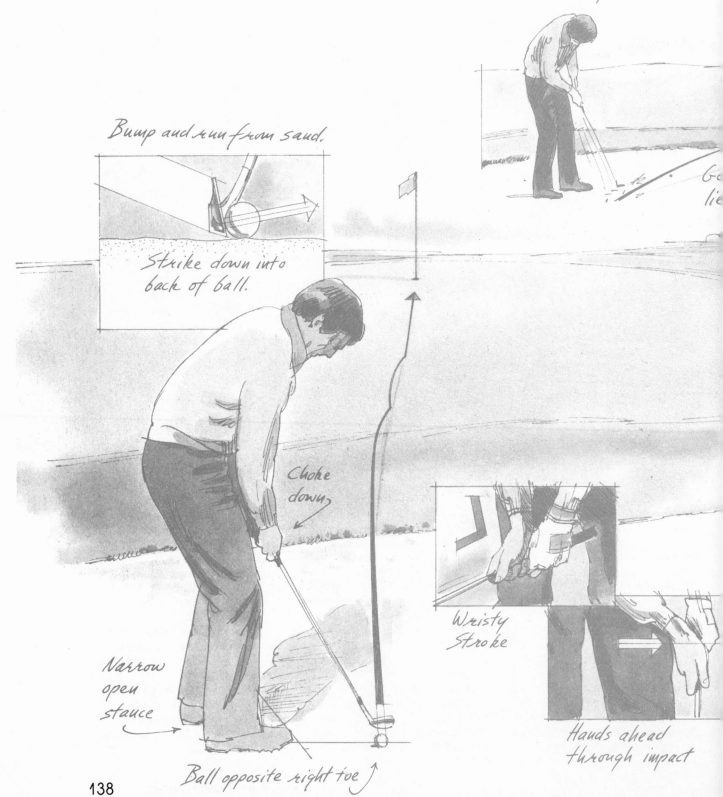

6

TO BLAST OR
NOT TO BLAST

Putt out of a trap when the pin is cut close to the edge of the green.

Bump and run from sand.

Strike down into back of ball.

Choke down

Wristy Stroke

Narrow open stance

Ball opposite right toe

Hands ahead through impact

As a low handicapper, you probably have a good sand game. You may not be a wizard, but you know how to play the basic explosion shot so the ball stops reasonably close to the hole.

← Low lip

Woodworking Drill

Chipping off sand requires hitting the ball before hitting sand. Practice this at home by chipping balls off a piece of wood or off your garage or basement floor with an old club. If you don't hit the ball first, you'll be in trouble — the clubhead will bounce and belly the ball.

But blasting isn't always your only option from a greenside bunker. Under some conditions, chipping or even putting from a sand trap betters your chance of getting the ball close. How do you know which shot to use? How do you play them? Here's how.

BUMP-AND-RUN FROM SAND
Playing from greenside sand means you must carry the lip of the bunker, usually by blasting the ball and flying it most of the way to the pin. However, the percentages are in your favor whenever you can reduce the shot's air time and let it roll on the green most of the way to the hole. The following conditions must be met if you choose a bump-and-run shot from sand.

First, there should be little or no lip. The bump-and-run should fly on a low trajectory, not float over a mound.

Second, the pin should be well back. If it's close to the trap, play the explosion.

Third, the ball should sit up on the surface. You have to hit the ball first, which gets tougher the deeper the ball is in the sand.

To play the shot, position the ball opposite your right toe, improving your chances of hitting it before the sand. Playing the ball this far back reduces the loft of the club, so take one more than you need—for example, a 9-iron rather than an 8. Choke down on the club, angle your hands ahead of the ball and take a narrow, open stance.

Keep the head and body still and make a wristy stroke, hitting down into the back of the ball, the hands leading the blade through impact. The shot should have some backspin, making it bite on the first bounce before releasing, so hit it a little harder than if you were playing from grass.

PUTTING FROM SAND
The best time to putt out of a trap is when the pin is cut close to the edge of the green, making a short blast or chip a tricky venture. Putt only if the lie is good and the trap has little or no lip.

The stroke you want is a long, smooth, arms-and-shoulders motion, the kind you would make for a long approach putt. Play the ball a little more forward in your stance than usual so you contact it slightly on the upswing; hitting with a downward blow only pushes the ball further into the sand. Set your weight slightly toward your heels at address, again to avoid hitting the sand before the ball on the forward swing.

In gauging the force of the stroke, remember that sand is slower than grass, so give the ball some extra juice.

Finally, with any trap shot, never touch the sand with the clubhead at address. Hover it behind the ball to prevent a two-shot penalty.

7

HONE YOUR VISUALIZATION

Take a moment before you set up to "see" the ball flight you want.

As you prepare to play your shot, are you still thinking about certain mechanical elements of the stroke? Your takeaway, your top-of-backswing position, your down-swing move?

Don't! At this point in your shot preparation, you must put mechanics behind you and focus your attention on the target—whether it's the garden spot in the fairway for a drive or the center of the hole for a putt. Jack Nicklaus is famous for his visualization system, and it's worth adopting for your own game, too.

Using a spot technique at address brings the target closer to you.

He begins by standing behind the ball, waiting until he "sees" in his mind's eye the exact flight of the ball that he wants. Only after he has "seen" the entire shot does he step up to the ball and, after settling in, set in motion his meticulous target-alignment system. His eyes focus on one of several intermediate points along the target line and back to the ball, on the next intermediate point and back and so on. Focusing on these points assures him that his clubface is perfectly aligned with his target. Just before he is ready to take his club back, Nicklaus again sees a vivid image of his shot flying unerringly toward his target.

Through this image process, Nicklaus erases any negative thoughts and gives himself the greatest possible chance of putting his excellent mechanics to work.

Try to develop your own preshot routine following Jack's model. Before stepping up to the ball, see in your mind's eye the way the shot should fly. If you want to draw your tee shot away from trouble on the right, stand behind the ball and watch the shot take off on a low line before rising and curving gradually left. If you need to fade a soft iron shot to a pin tucked tightly on the right side, visualize that curving pattern. Then develop checkpoints that help you set up to achieve that flight pattern and direction.

If you can draw the shot clearly enough in your mind before addressing the ball, your subconscious will help you program the body. Trust your subconscious and see if the results don't surprise you.

8

UP AND DOWN FROM "OPEN" ROUGH

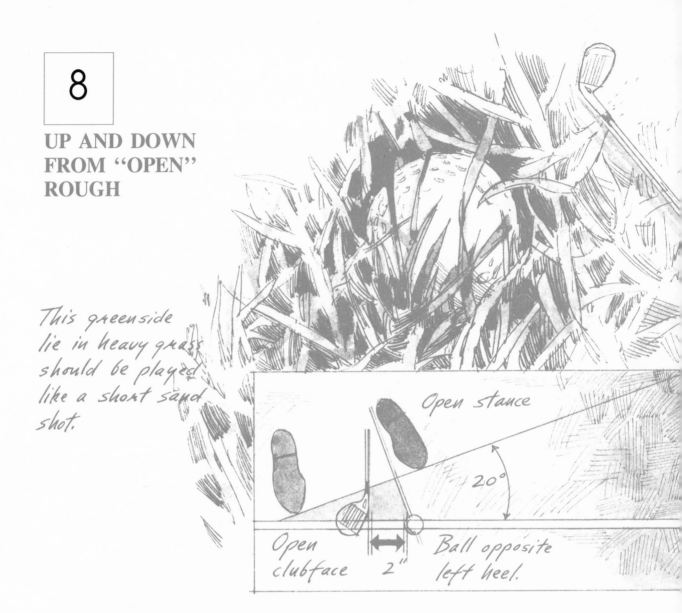

This greenside lie in heavy grass should be played like a short sand shot.

Open stance

20°

Open clubface

2"

Ball opposite left heel.

Every now and then, especially on tough courses, you miss a green, the ball finishes in deep greenside rough and you fail to get up and down because you have trouble hitting a soft chip shot. If that's so, you need the secret to a steady recovery. Running the ball past the hole isn't good enough when the match is on the line, so here's how to hit softly out of the rough.

OPEN THE ANGLES
Assuming there's not much green to work with, use your sand-shot technique out of the long grass. You don't want to strike the ball, but hit behind it the way you would on a short bunker shot, lofting the ball out so it stops near the hole.

Like the short sand shot, you

address the ball with a slightly open stance, setting the blade of the sand wedge open by about 20 degrees. (Always use the sand wedge, not the pitching wedge, since you want the club to glide through the grass rather than dig.) The open stance promotes an outside-in cutting action that helps pop the ball, while the open blade adds loft to the club. Play the ball opposite your left heel. Hover the clubhead a few inches behind the ball since you intend to hit that far behind it. Light grip pressure allows a wristy, U-shaped swing.

RIGHT SIDE CONTROLS THE SHOT
The proper feel for this shot is a slicing action controlled by the

right hand. Start the club back with a slight cocking of the right wrist so the clubhead comes up quickly. The length of the backswing varies with the length of the shot and the depth of the grass, but swinging back a touch farther than you think necessary will promote a smooth tempo because you won't be tempted to accelerate the swing for more power.

Your right hand and forearm activate the downswing; you should feel a slight throwing or casting motion as the first move down. This allows a slicing or slapping action through the grass, hitting about two inches behind the ball with the club moving in the steeper, U-shaped arc. As you make this outside-in slicing motion, keep

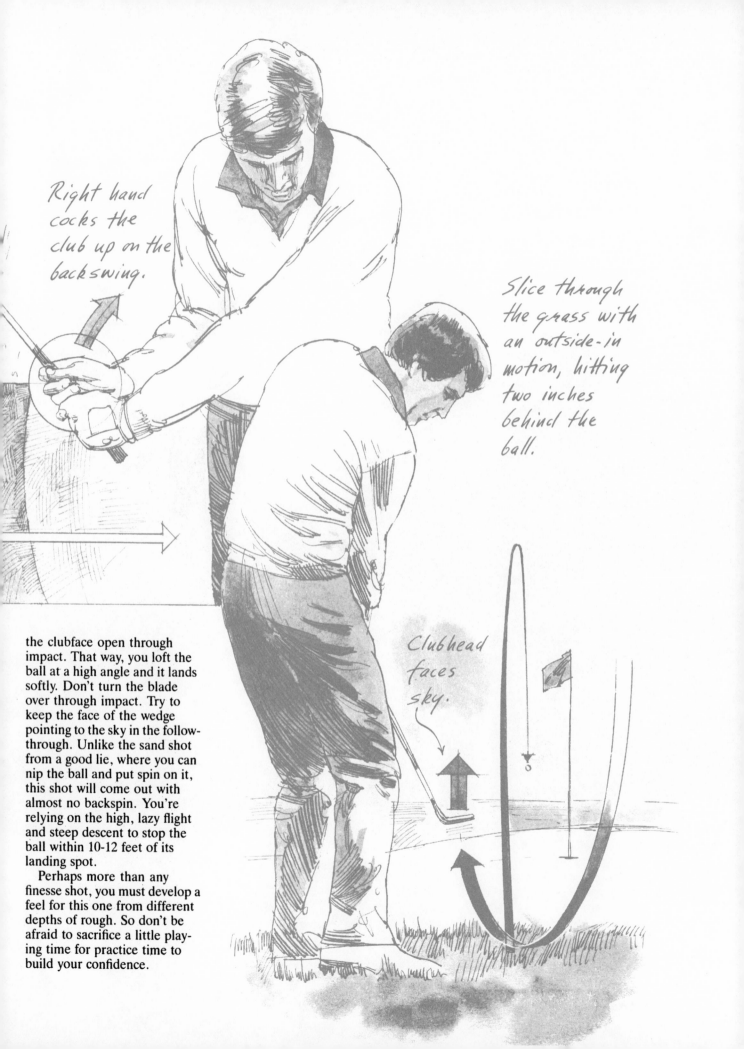

Right hand cocks the club up on the backswing.

Slice through the grass with an outside-in motion, hitting two inches behind the ball.

Clubhead faces sky.

the clubface open through impact. That way, you loft the ball at a high angle and it lands softly. Don't turn the blade over through impact. Try to keep the face of the wedge pointing to the sky in the follow-through. Unlike the sand shot from a good lie, where you can nip the ball and put spin on it, this shot will come out with almost no backspin. You're relying on the high, lazy flight and steep descent to stop the ball within 10-12 feet of its landing spot.

Perhaps more than any finesse shot, you must develop a feel for this one from different depths of rough. So don't be afraid to sacrifice a little play-ing time for practice time to build your confidence.

9

WHAT KIND OF
DAY WILL IT BE?

If warm-up shots move mostly from right-to-left, plan on playing a draw.

Despite your highly respectable handicap, your swing is not set in stone the way a pro's is. You, therefore, cannot deliver the clubface to the ball in precisely the same way every time. On some days, you contact the ball with a slightly open face, imparting fadespin on the ball. Other days, the face arrives slightly closed and you hit mostly draws.

To determine the kind of shots you'll hit on any given day, start your round on the practice tee. Hit a couple dozen practice balls, particularly with woods and long to medium irons, to see how the ball is moving, right-to-left or left-to-right. Once you know, prepare yourself to rely on that shot throughout that day.

PUTTING CHANGES, TOO
If you're like most golfers, the putter also feels different from day to day. Some rounds you have a good feel for distance, other days you can't miss reading breaks. It's important to practice putting before the round and identify the day's strengths.

If your confidence is high on short putts, be aggressive on long putts. If, however, you feel tentative over the three-to-four footers, putt defensively; concentrate on lagging the ball close to avoid three putting.

Identify what your putting strengths are for that day on the practice green.

10

MAKE THOSE "MONEY" PUTTS

Every golfer fears the "yips"—that horrible condition when your putting stroke regresses into a nervous twitch and you become a shambles at the thought of even a three footer. The yips don't suddenly hit you like the flu; first you miss some easy putts, then you begin doubting your stroke. Before you know it, your confidence has crumbled, and every putt is a gut-wrencher. So if the short ones are sliding by more often than they're dropping, it's time to cure the problem before it gets worse.

CHECK YOUR ALIGNMENT

Most cases of erratic putting from short range begin with faulty alignment. You probably aren't aiming properly, so the putts aren't rolling where you want them to.

A good way to check your aim is by putting over an intermediate target. Set up for a three-foot putt and put a ball marker on the putting line about six inches in front of the ball. Align the putterhead to stroke the ball over the marker. Look at the cup: If you feel as if you're aiming to the right or left of it, that's a good indication your aim is off.

Hit several balls ignoring the hole and aiming over the marker. The putts should start dropping. After a dozen or so, focus on the cup but continue aiming at the marker. After holing some more putts, pick up the marker and concentrate only on the hole. You now should have a good sense of when you're correctly aimed at the hole.

Although you can't place a marker in front of your ball while playing, you can use an intermediate target. Look for a spot on the ground or blade of grass on the line and aim at it.

ACCELERATE!

Short-putt problems on the green also might be the result of a tentative stroke. The more you miss, the greater the tendency to decelerate on the forward stroke. This leads to a wobbly swing path, causing pushed or pulled putts.

No matter how short the putt, you must accelerate the club through the ball. To get the feel of the proper stroke, practice from short range, taking the putter back only half as far as normal and exaggerating the follow-through by keeping the putterface on line and moving the blade straight toward the cup. This practice can work wonders restoring your putting stroke and confidence.

Check your alignment by using an intermediate marker.

Intermediate marker.

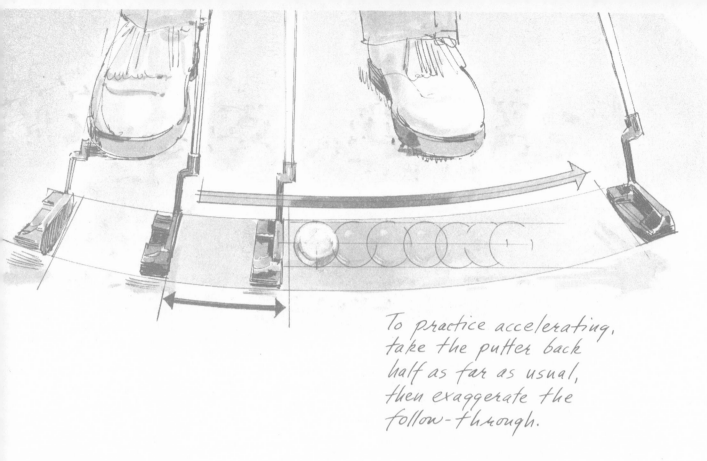

To practice accelerating, take the putter back half as far as usual, then exaggerate the follow-through.

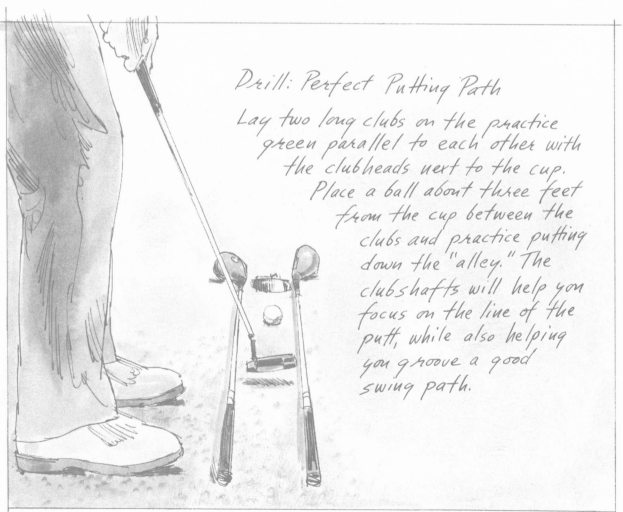

Drill: Perfect Putting Path

Lay two long clubs on the practice green parallel to each other with the clubheads next to the cup. Place a ball about three feet from the cup between the clubs and practice putting down the "alley." The clubshafts will help you focus on the line of the putt, while also helping you groove a good swing path.

11

BEWARE GAMESMANSHIP

Most golfers in competition concentrate on playing their games while letting the opposition play theirs. But some opponents will try to gain an advantage by acting in a way designed to distract the golfer from his game and influence his thoughts and strategies. This ploy is called "gamesmanship."

Walter Hagen was a master gamesman who cut down the competition by exaggerating the confidence he had in his game. In one instance, Hagen and his opponent faced short putts for par. Preparing to putt first, Hagen snickered, then explained that he was thinking how long his foe's putt was going to look after he had made his. Hagen

"This green is a lot slower than the others."

"There's a lot of wind up there."

smartly rapped his home.

Whenever you encounter gamesmanship, the best procedure is to ignore it. Here's what to look for and advice for sticking to your game.

MAKE YOUR OWN DECISIONS

Sometimes what sounds like a casual comment is actually a stratagem to undermine your game. For example, after your opponent mishits a putt, leaving it well short, he might make a remark about "this green being a lot slower than the others." He's hoping you'll take his comment seriously enough to hit your putt hard and run it well beyond the hole.

Or after fading an approach right of the green, he may glance at the sky and say, "There's a lot of wind up there," trying to throw off your approach. Make up your own mind when planning a shot and stick with it. If you do make a mistake, make sure it is *your* mistake, not someone else's doing.

WATCH PACE OF PLAY

A more subtle form of gamesmanship involves pace of play. An opponent can sense when you've found a good playing rhythm. He may speed up or slow down his own pace, hoping to affect yours.

He may begin taking more or less time than usual over each shot.

If you notice his pace changing, don't be taken in: Continue playing at a pace comfortable for you. Once he realizes you're not fooled by his antics, you've gained the edge.

Watch out for him creeping into your vision, standing right behind you and in your line of sight while you address a shot or walking well ahead as you get ready to hit. If you're distracted, ask him to move.

If you're aware that gamesmanship is being practiced on you, take it as a compliment. It means your opponent feels he needs it to beat you. Gain some confidence, forget your opponent's tricks and play your own game.

If an opponent distracts you visually, ask him to move.

Slowing the pace

12

"SUCKER" PIN PLACEMENTS

You swing the club with the skill to hit the ball solidly and accurately, but if you're hitting fewer than 10 greens per round, you may be getting "suckered in" by pin placements.

WHAT IS A SUCKER PIN?
A "sucker pin" is one that has been positioned to lull you into taking unnecessary risks on the approach. Whether or not a pin is in a sucker spot depends on your natural shot. Suppose that shot is a fade, and the hole you're playing

Going for a "Sucker" Pin demands that you flirt with missing the green.

has a heavily bunkered green, with the pin cut close to the left edge. Being an aggressive player, you're planning to hit it stiff for a possible birdie. Rather than play your fade into the wealth of green to the right of the pin, you start the ball toward the sand on the left, hoping to cut it in close. If you pull it off, great; if not, you're now trying to get up and down from the trap to save par.

If a draw is your natural shot, the pin on the left side of the green isn't in a sucker position. You can aim to the fat of the green and work the ball back to the pin. If the ball doesn't move, you're still safely on the dance floor.

DON'T BE TAKEN IN
Although you know it makes sense to play toward the safe part of the green, it's easy to abandon the smart play when you're standing in the fairway, the ball is sitting up, you're holding a middle iron and the flag beckons in the distance. That's the moment to tell yourself, "Don't be suckered!"

Try this experiment: Force yourself to play a round taking the conservative route on all approach shots. If going for the flag means giving away the green or aiming close to the edge, don't try it. Don't shoot for the flag but for the middle of the green. Imagine another pin is there—a "safety" pin—and aim for that. Your odds of getting on the green rise, giving you a good chance for at least a two-putt par, and there's still the possibility of sinking a long putt for birdie.

Exercise caution by imagining a "safety" pin and playing to that instead.

13

THE KNOCKDOWN WEDGE

You're a good enough player to execute a choice of wedge shots from 70 to 110 yards out. But can you hit a "knockdown" wedge? This low, checking shot is both safe and fun to play.

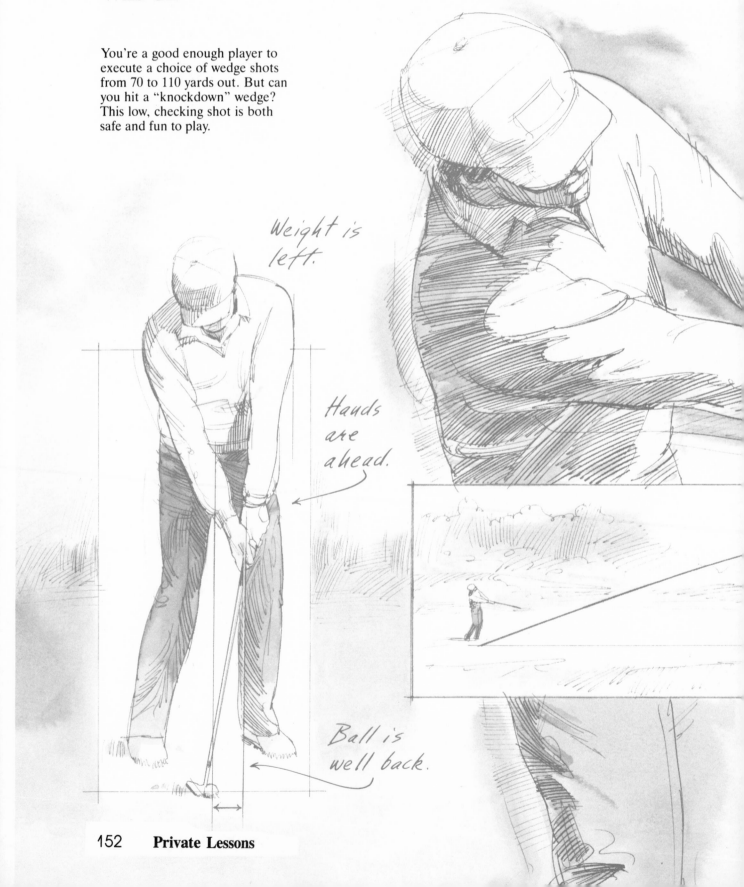

Weight is left.

Hands are ahead.

Ball is well back.

WHEN TO PLAY IT

Whenever the pin is toward the back of the green, so there's plenty of room in front, go with the knockdown wedge, especially if there's trouble over the green. The knockdown also is a savior on a windy day when gusts would kill a high shot.

The knockdown wedge has two advantages: 1) It's easy to hit solidly, and 2) It's easy to control the distance because you're not trying to fly the ball all the way to the hole and make it stop. But you can play it only from a good fairway lie or hardpan, where the ball can be trapped between the clubface and the ground to get spin. If you have a flyer lie, play a conventional wedge while allowing for more carry and roll.

HOW TO PLAY IT

The knockdown works with either the pitching or sand wedge. The pitching wedge is safer because the smaller flange is less likely to catch the ground first, even from a tight lie.

Set the leading edge of the clubface square to the target and take a fairly narrow, slightly open stance. Your hands should be well ahead of the ball, most of your weight on your left foot, and the ball back of center. This setup encourages the descending blow you need.

Choke down slightly to reduce the arc of the clubhead and help keep the ball down. Your grip should be firm, particularly with your left hand.

Make an arm swing, pushing the club straight back without consciously cocking the wrists. As you swing to the top, a little weight may move to the inside of your right foot, but not much. Swing the club up as far as you need for the shot at hand but never past three-quarter length. A big swing will get the ball higher in the air so if you need more distance than you can get from the wedge with a three-quarter swing, drop down to a 9-iron.

Pull down and through the ball with your left hand and arm. The sharp "thunk" means you've hit the ball on the downswing, maybe even a little high on the ball, which is okay for a low shot.

At the finish, your arms and the club should point at the target. Even though the swing is abbreviated, the shot will travel a little farther than you think because the club has been delofted.

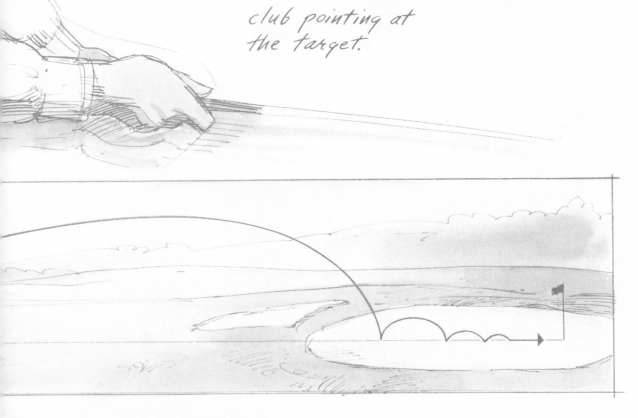

Finish with the club pointing at the target.

With the pin back and plenty of green, go with the knockdown wedge.

14

ESCAPE FROM
THE BACK LIP

Use pitching wedge.

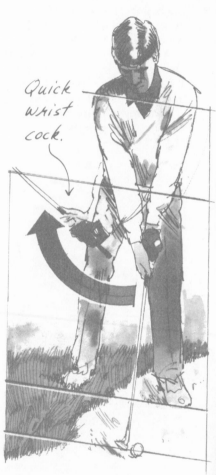

Quick whrist cock.

Pick club up quickly with hands on a very vertical plane.

Choke down on grip.

Mainly an "arms" swing.

Follow-through will be limited.

Drill

To practice the proper steep swing needed to escape from the back lip of a bunker, place a ball about three feet from the trunk of a tree and practice hitting shots with the tree restricting the arc of your swing.

When a course situation or lie is particularly severe, even par shooters like you must bite the bullet and play for bogey. Remember: You can make amends for a bogey, but it's tough getting back to level par after scoring a "triple." So in facing a challenging lie, play more with your head and less with your heart.

One of the most challenging of these positions is freeing a ball from just inside the back lip of a sand trap. The problem is obvious: Because the lip is so close behind the ball, you must execute an extremely steep swing, almost an up-and-down chopping motion. Making this shot requires some changes in technique.

Club selection: With such a steep swing, the large flange of the sand wedge probably will bounce off the sand and belly the ball, so take the pitching wedge. Its smaller flange cuts more easily into the sand, sliding under the ball and lifting it out.

Stance: You may have to stand with the right foot out of the bunker, the left foot in. Don't twist the left foot too deeply into the sand or your hips and shoulders won't be parallel to the ground you're standing on. So dig in just enough to prevent slipping.

Swing: To avoid hitting the lip on the backswing, the club must be picked up quickly with the hands, which you do by gripping lightly in the fingers and choking down on the shaft almost to the metal. Begin the backswing with a quick wrist cock so the club travels on a vertical plane. Don't worry if the club seems to be moving back on a drastically outside-in swing path; this is natural.

Plan to contact the sand about half-an-inch behind the ball, taking less sand than you would on a normal explosion shot. Think "down and through" at impact. There won't be much follow-through because of the steep downswing, but concentrating on one will help you accelerate the clubhead, which is essential to successfully freeing the ball.

Swing with the arms, keeping the lower body quiet. Any lower-body movement toward the target before impact increases the risk of blading the ball.

Strategy: Play conservatively. When it's almost impossible to get the club on a ball that is either buried or touching the lip, it might be best to play out sideways or even backwards. A bogey might be a good score from such a position, and this strategy should keep one bad lie from ruining an entire round.

15

DRIVE, DON'T STEER

Take a deep breath and relax.

Arms free of tension.

Grip is light in the fingers.

Even skilled players tighten up when they see a particularly narrow fairway, then try to "steer" the shot by making a slower, shorter swing. You may think restricting the swing gives you more control, but it doesn't.

While trying to steer a shot, you generally tense up and think about making a shorter, slower swing that allows you to guide the clubhead straight through the ball, producing a straight shot.

Whether or not you're conscious of the changes in your swing and preparation, the results are sure to be bad. A slower swing means less clubhead speed, but worse, it may result in deceleration through impact. Or because you're not used to swinging at a reduced speed, your timing may go off, and the straight shot you're so desperate for becomes a hook or a slice.

There are ways to put a little more control into your drives while still making your normal, aggressive swing.

PRIORITY #1: RELAX
It's natural to feel some pressure when staring down a tree-lined fairway or at some other hazard-prone predicament. So your first concern must be to relax: Take a deep breath, remember that you're a good player with the ability to hit the ball straight and safe, and keep cool. You want every part of your body to be at ease, but pay special attention to your hands and arms: Make sure your grip is light in the fingers and your arms are free of tension.

It's impossible to guide the clubhead through the shot from start to finish, so don't even try. Trust that your normal setup and swing will move the club properly through the ball.

GAIN CONTROL IN OTHER WAYS
You can add control by making changes that don't disturb your swing rhythm. Choking up an inch or two on the club slows your swing naturally, without creating tension.

Making a three-quarter swing will cost you a little distance, but if you don't unnaturally slow the rhythm, will lead to a straighter shot.

Consider dropping down to a 3-wood or even an iron; again, you might lose distance, but the more lofted clubs won't put as much sidespin on the ball, leading to a straighter shot.

Whatever steps you take, relax over the ball and make your normal, aggressive swing. Let the shot "happen" instead of trying to *make* it happen.

Make an aggressive swing and _let_ the shot "happen."

SURVIVING A SLUMP

Suddenly you feel like you can't do anything right.

Every player, regardless of skill, is going to have his share of bad days. Although playing poorly is no fun, usually you can get back on track the next time out and quickly forget the bad round.

Sometimes, though, one bad day runs into another and another. Before you know it, you're in a slump.

A slump is a self-fulfilling prophecy. The game that seemed simple a week ago suddenly is a mystery. The backslide may start with the long game, which puts additional pressure on your short game to salvage a decent score. But few players can live on chipping and putting alone so that part of your game soon starts showing the effects of your crumbling confidence—now that you can't do anything right—and there seems no end in sight. Or your short game may be the first to suffer, which puts pressure on your tee-to-green game. Whatever goes first, you'll end up in the same place—a slump.

The first step in shaking off a slump is to mentally shake yourself out. You've shot low scores before, so you know you're capable of better. Bring a confident outlook to your problem-solving.

GET BACK TO BASICS
Ball-striking goes awry when some problem has crept into your fundamentals. Start at address. Check to see that even the smallest ingredient is correct: Body alignment, ball position, weight distribution. Maybe you've moved too close to the ball without realizing it. Or your grip has turned too strong or too weak. Examine every element of address.

USE YOUR KNOWLEDGE
You know a fair amount about the swing, so you probably have made a few educated guesses already. For example, you may be pulling the ball, which is caused by an outside-in downswing path. The problem might be an outside-in takeaway or coming over the top on the downswing. By examining the effects, you can step backward through the swing and look for the causes.

But if your slump doesn't respond to self-examination, seek out a teaching pro for help.

Stay Healthy (Drill)

Another old saying is "an ounce of prevention is worth a pound of cure." You can keep bad habits from forming by regularly monitoring your fundamentals. During pre-round warm-ups, lay a club down across your feet to check alignment, and another club perpendicular to the first to check ball position. By preventing pre-swing faults, you'll also prevent the swing faults that result from them.

If a slump persists, seek the expert advice of a pro.

17

THE HATED
HALF-WEDGE

Make a smooth rhythmic swing going back and coming through.

Mainly an arms swing.

You break 80 fairly regularly, but there still are a few shots you don't have in your bag. How many times have you hit two solid shots on a long par five to within 50 yards of the green, then followed them with a mediocre wedge to 25 feet and a two-putt par? If you could hit a soft, accurate half-wedge, your birdies would multiply.

A delicate wedge also can keep trouble at bay. Say you're in trouble off the tee on a par four. You have to settle for getting your second shot close to, but not on, the green. A little flipped wedge close to the hole can turn bogey into par. If you don't know this scoring shot, now's the time to learn.

DISTANCE WITH FINESSE
Many players have difficulty with shots hit at less than full power because they don't know the proper technique for a finesse shot that travels more than just a few yards. A wedge hit full-force is easy: Set up, take it back and pull the trigger. But when distance is not the goal, the tendency is to take a full backswing, then decelerate coming down, leaving the ball way short of the target—often in a greenside hazard. Another mistake is making an abrupt, "handsy"

To add more hand action, allow your wrists to hinge properly on the backswing.

Lighten grip pressure.

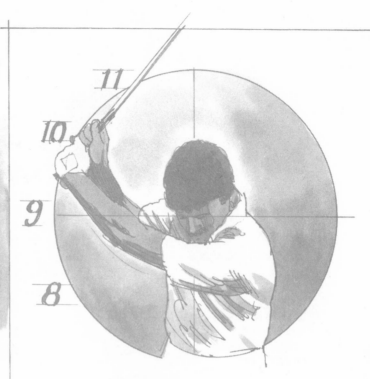

backswing, then chopping down on the ball. That shot can fly in any direction.

The key to hitting the half-wedge is a smooth swing back and through. The arms make the motion, so keep the lower body still. Don't slow down the down-swing; keep the swing fluid and accelerate through the ball.

HANDS-ON METHOD

Hitting a crisp half-wedge requires a little more hand action than the amount needed for a full-swing shot. To get the hands working, lighten your grip pressure at address, which will allow your wrists to hinge faster on the backswing. Keep a relaxed, but firm, hold on the club; the hands will work naturally in your favor as you hit down on the shot, provid-ing crisp contact between blade and ball.

The 10'Clock Wedge Drill

To get the feel for hitting less-than-full wedge shots, practice gauging the length of your backswing. Practice taking your hands back to the ten o'clock position on the backswing and accelerating through the ball from there. Measure how far you average hitting the ball from the ten o'clock position—say it's fifty yards. Now you have a point to work from. To hit shorter, bring the hands back slightly less than ten o'clock; for longer shots, bring them slightly past, accelerating at the same smooth pace on every one.

18

SEE THE LINE

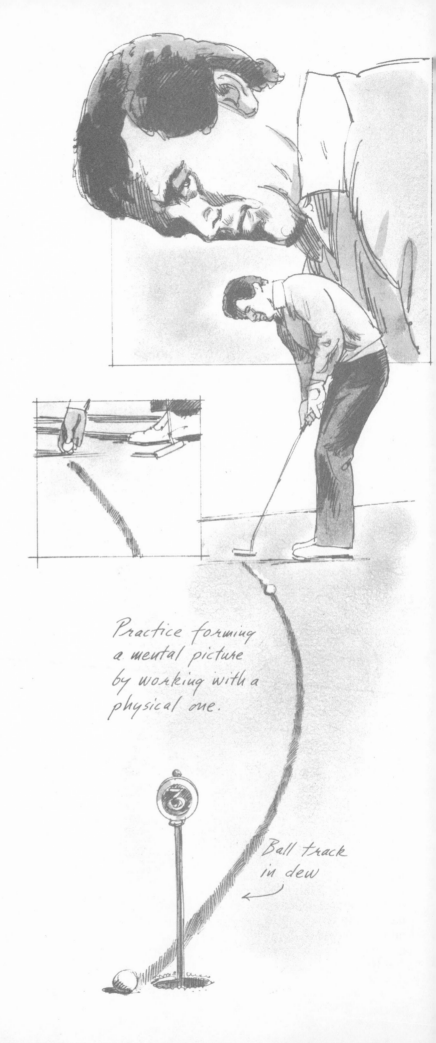

You've probably heard a lot about the importance of visualizing a shot before playing it: Imagining how it will feel coming off the club and how it will look flying to the target. "Seeing" the shot is an important part of the preshot routine of most skilled players.

Visualization shouldn't stop when you reach the green. Being able to "see" the line the ball will take is sure to help you. If every putt were straight, picturing the line wouldn't be hard (for that matter, neither would putting), but as you know, it's a rare putt that doesn't have some break to it. If you're having trouble seeing the line, this lesson is for you.

SHARPEN YOUR FOCUS
Practice forming a good mental picture by working with a physical picture first. Get to the practice green while it's still covered with dew. Find a place where the dew is untouched and stroke a 15 footer. Leave the path the first ball cuts untouched and place another ball at its head. Stand behind this ball as if reading a putt and concentrate on the line, then step up to the ball, glance at the line one more time and stroke the ball. Repeat this twice more, then move five feet closer to the cup and go through the same procedure with three more putts on the same line. Move five feet closer and hit three five footers, all the time ingraining the image of the line in your mind.

Practice forming a mental picture by working with a physical one.

Ball track in dew

EYES OVER THE LINE

You'll have a better chance of seeing a line if your eyes are directly over it. To find out if yours are positioned properly, address a putt, then without moving your feet, place two balls next to the original—one directly in front, the other in back. Without your putter, assume your address again and bring a ball up so it touches the bridge of your nose (between your eyes). Let it drop straight down. If it hits any of the three balls, your eyes are over the line. If not, adjust yourself until you can pass this test.

Drop a ball from the bridge of your nose to see if your eyes are over the line.

Down the Line Drill

If you aren't out early enough to catch the dew, you can still practice seeing the line. Stroke a fifteen-foot putt, carefully observing its line. Place five balls along the line, three feet apart. Stroke the one closest to the hole, then quickly go to the next and strike it, keeping the path of the last putt clearly in mind.

19

TEE TALK

A round of golf played in regulation rewards you with 54 perfect lies: 36 putts (two per green) and 18 tee shots. On the green, you must play the ball where it lays, but on the tee you can place it exactly how and where you want. So while you're deciding on what type of shot to hit, think carefully about the best placement of the ball in the teeing ground.

USE THE FULL DEPTH
The Rules of golf require players to tee off from between the markers. But you have more latitude than you might think.

Don't let habit keep you from using the whole teeing area.

Depth of two clublengths

The teeing area is defined by two markers, but isn't confined to the straight line running between them. The actual teeing ground is the rectangle formed by the width between the markers and by the depth of two clublengths.

On par-four and five holes, you probably tee off as far forward as possible to get every inch of driving distance. On par threes, however, moving around within the allowed rectangle will let you make precise adjustments in direction and distance.

Having a little leeway can make life easier when you are having difficulty deciding between two clubs; instead of standing all the way forward and trying to swing easy—with the risk of letting up on the shot—set up farther back and swing fully. Although the distance from the front to the back line is little more than two yards, the psychological lift of being farther away should encourage you to make an aggressive shot, accelerating through the downswing.

Use the full width of the rectangle as well. Only the ball is required to be within the teeing area; the player may stand outside. A right-handed player can tee the ball along the left edge of the rectangle and address it with his feet outside of the box.

TEEING TIPS

How you tee the ball also can make a big difference on par threes where conditions call for a particular kind of approach shot. Pulling it off might be easier if you tee the ball up in something other than your usual manner.

For example, say you want the ball to land at the front of the green and run to the back. In that case, you'd set up for an intentional "flyer" by kicking up a small tuft of grass with your heel and placing the ball just in front of it. This will get a few blades of grass between the clubface and the ball at impact, which will reduce the backspin on the shot so it releases quickly and runs after landing.

If there's a tailwind, tee the ball a little higher than usual to catch it farther up on the clubface. This produces a higher-flying shot that will ride the wind to the target and stop quickly when it hits.

Against the wind, tee the ball a little lower than usual to hit a shot with a lower trajectory that stays under the wind.

One final tip: Don't assume that the tee area is flat. There may be subtle undulations that can throw off your shot. Besides checking the ground around where you place the ball, check around your feet. Be sure the area is flat, your feet are level with the ball and your footing is secure.

Also check that the tee markers aim straight down the fairway. If not, they could point you toward trouble. This misdirection could be the architect's little joke or the greenkeeper's oversight; either way, don't depend on the markers when setting up.

Only the ball has to be within the boundaries.

20

SPLASH!

Quick wrist break

Close blade of wedge

Half the ball is visible above the surface.

Take solid, open stance, with ball played just left of center.

Your approach shot has come down along the edge of a green-side pond. When you get to the spot, you see it sitting in shallow water but close enough to the edge that you think you have a shot. Your first thought is to hit out of the hazard to avoid a penalty stroke.

But wait a minute. Calm down and carefully assess your options. A good recovery will save you the penalty stroke, but an unsuccessful shot will mean more wasted strokes—to say nothing of wet clothes and a dampened spirit.

The decision whether or not to play out of the water will be influ-

Come down briskly.

enced by two factors: How much of the ball is submerged, and whether you can take a steady stance.

THE LIE
Never attempt to hit out of water unless at least half the ball is above the surface. Any less than that means you'll have to move the clubhead through too much water; you won't have any power left by the time the club meets the ball, and the water may turn the clubface so it is too open or closed at impact.

THE STANCE
Resurrecting a ball from a watery grave requires an aggressive swing, so you must set up in a stable, secure stance, even if you have to take off a shoe and step into the water. Without at least one foot shod and on the ground, the stance probably won't be very solid, and you shouldn't chance the shot.

THE SHOT
The lie and stance are favorable. You hit the shot the way you would from a buried lie in the sand, with an upright swing and a descending blow.

Use a pitching wedge, because that club features a high degree of loft and has a sharp leading edge. Assume an open stance and play the ball midway between your feet. Close the blade of the wedge to help it cut easily through the water. As in sand, you may not ground the club in the hazard, so be careful not to touch the water with the clubhead while address-ing the ball.

Break your wrists quickly on the backswing. Then pull the club swiftly down into a spot directly behind the ball; tentativeness will wreck your chances of getting out. Once you've decided to attempt the shot, stay with it. Deceleration on the downswing will destroy any hope of blasting free. Finally, don't flinch from the spray of water at contact: There's no sense getting wet unless you're going to get the ball out, so stay with it.

Low Handicapper 167

21

DRIVER FROM THE FAIRWAY

In certain situations, hitting the driver off the fairway is a smart play for the low handicapper: for example, a fairly open par five just out of 3-wood range or into a strong wind when you need all the distance you can get.

You need the right conditions, in particular, the lie must be good—the top of the ball at least level with the top of your soled driver. The deeper your clubface, therefore, the better the lie you'll need. (If you carry a metal driver, you might be able to use it from a slightly tighter lie. Experiment to find its limits.) If the ball's sitting up in light rough with a nice cushion underneath, it'll be easier to hit than from off the fairway.

The key is to contact the ball at the exact bottom of the swing: So, if you catch your drives a touch on the upswing as you should, play the ball a bit back in your stance from where you play the tee shot—just inside the left heel.

A wide, shallow swing arc is a must. Push the club back very low and slow, with no deliberate wrist cock during the backswing. Most of your weight flows onto your right side at the top. Start down as usual by shifting your weight onto your left foot. However, strive to keep your head back a bit through impact. Staying "behind the ball" ensures a shallow clubhead path and a level hit.

Good technique is more important than muscle. Don't try to "lift" the shot. Stay with it, extending the club low to the ground well past impact. ■

Low takeaway with wrists firm aids sweeping action with the driver.